What is it that impels men like Niki Lauda?
Or that makes him and his fellow drivers,
James Hunt, Jody Scheckter, Patrick
Depailler, Emerson Fittipaldi and a host of
others, put their lives on the line in the
world's most dangerous sport?
Niki Lauda's dedication to racing almost
ended at the Nurburgring circuit in August
1976, but he has fought his way back against
incredible odds to maintain his position
at the peak of his career. This book tells
his story, and opens up the glamorous,
perilous and totally enthralling world of
Formula 1 racing. A world which, for
champions like Niki Lauda, is an
all-embracing way of life.

Niki Lauda and the Grand Prix Gladiators

A Biography by RONNIE MUTCH

SPHERE BOOKS LIMITED
30/32 Gray's Inn Road, London WC1X 8JL

First published in Great Britain by
Sphere Books Ltd. 1977
Copyright © Ronnie Mutch 1977

TRADE
MARK

Set in Intertype Plantin

Printed in Great Britain by
Hunt Barnard Printing Ltd.,
Aylesbury, Bucks.

CONTENTS

ACKNOWLEDGEMENTS

My grateful thanks to:

David Armstrong for help and some photographs.

Mal Currie, Race Director Watkins Glen, for help and attention.

John Surtees of Surtees Racing, for time and attention.

Alan Walters and Mauro Forghieri for instruction on the niceties of F1 racers.

Ermanno Coughi for instruction on the niceties of F1 mechanics.

Max Mosley of March Engineering, for interesting, thoughtful and accurate information.

Alan Radnor, Executive Editor Penthouse Publications, for help.

All the drivers, mechanics and officials who gave me unstintingly of their time at races.

James Hunt for his valuable time.

Mrs Gerger for the use of her apartment in Watkins Glen.

Elizabeth Radice for her unfailingly meticulous transcription of my scrawl.

Peter MacIntosh of F.I.C.A. for information.

Penny in Super Duper Watkins Glen, for smiling.

To my wife, Hilary, for her help and comments.

And finally Niki and Marlene – all happiness in your lives.

I

Niki Lauda

*Even now, after the accident, for me there is more on
the positive side of motor racing than the negative
side.* Niki Lauda.

I first saw him two months after his near fatal accident. He
eased himself carefully out of his flame red Ferrari, took off
his gloves and crash helmet and lifted his flame-proof mask.
'I need more downthrust. More wing.'
He spoke in English to the chief designer of the Ferrari
Formula One team, Mauro Forghieri. The photographers
zoomed in on his face with their long lenses. The clicks were
a faint obscenity.
'O.K., we try, but I think not,' said Engineer Forghieri.
The cameras were now all around, recording the scarred
death mask of a face for posterity. One member of the large
Ferrari team spoke to Niki.
'They are taking your photograph.'
Something which for reasons outside Niki's own feelings,
the team man wanted stopped. Bad public relations to ex-
pose the face? Not an up-market image for Ferrari? Niki
looked evenly at him.
'So they are taking photographs. Let them.' He turned to
his chief mechanic adjusting the aerofoil. 'Not too much.'
The mechanic, Ermanno Coughi, nodded, never taking
his eyes off the job on hand. The cameras clicked on. This is
something Niki Lauda has to live with now. Once he had a

smiley face, a big buck-toothed grin that would crack, not only when he was on the winners' podium, but at those personal moments when he found something amusing, which were frequent. Now there were fewer smiles.

His face and lungs were horribly burnt in his accident on the Nurburgring circuit on August 1, 1976. The accident jumped up on the television news all over the world. Niki Lauda, 1975 Formula One world champion, who looked like being world champion in 1976, beating our own beloved James Hunt in the process, had crashed. He was in a critical condition. Then, a day later, came the film. It was shot by an amateur and had all the ingredients of another amateur film which shocked the world light-years away, one day in 1962, when Emil Zapruder was filming President Kennedy in Dallas, Texas.

We are accustomed to the professional film shot for television – smooth pans, quick zoom-ins that frame the subject all the time. If you want slow motion the cameraman obligingly sets his speed to give everything in crisp detail. The amateur films of disaster are different. They switch on to take a few feet of some event to show their wives or friends and suddenly they are history's eyes. I have seen film from professional cameramen when they were facing certain death. The camera never flinched. It kept steady, the 'information' in perfect focus, aperture exact until the bullets smashed through the illusory magic of the camera or until the helicopter crashed. The amateur's instinct is for self. He will duck, run, flinch, all of which are natural and disastrous for the camera.

In the Lauda film the man was panning along with the speeding Ferrari when it happened. Slide and abrupt crash. He kept panning and the car disappeared. It took a second for the message to get through, then he panned back wildly – too wildly. Another car had slammed into the red Ferrari, then another. Then there were flames and Niki's co-competitors, now strange Martians with overlarge heads, ran up, were engulfed in flame, ran out and then ran back again.

Over everything there was flame and confusion. Then they replayed the film in slow motion, which blurred it; because of the absence of sound it was somehow more unnatural and more chilling. You saw Kennedy die, now you were watching Lauda in death's process, then the newsreader giving us the latest information on Lauda, politely intimating that his chances of survival were nil. At last, comfortable and comforting, professional film of the wreck and ambulances. All clear with synchronised sound. Now it was just another crash. On to the next bit of sanitised disaster. The news media over the next five days ignored Lauda, which is the usual occurrence presaging either death or disinterest. Niki, however, was alive. He was alive and knew precisely *what* had happened to him, although to this day not *how* it happened.

Fire, the devil's best friend, had caught him. It is fire that the racing driver fears most. You can slither, slide, roll or shunt – these they joke about, but about fire there are no jokes. You may walk away from a bad accident; very few people walk away from a fire and somewhere in every racing driver's memory is a picture of one of his friends, alive but beyond help, his life burning away in a storm of flame.

What happened to Niki was that he was trapped inside the cockpit of his Ferrari: something which happens very easily since the car is built around the driver, who sits with his legs stretched out in front of him with no space to spare ahead, sideways and behind, and hemmed in by two large petrol tanks. Under normal conditions it is difficult getting in and out of the cockpit. You cannot simply roll out. You have to release the safety harness and then heave yourself out. And when fire comes and the cockpit is ever so slightly distorted you are trapped in the middle of some forty gallons of high octane fuel.

A pole knocked Niki's crash helmet off and ripped the fireproof mask from his face. He was knocked out and continued to breathe normally, but what he breathed in was

11

not air, nor the emergency air supply connected to his lost helmet, but flame. And he breathed again and again. Finally the marshals got the extinguishers going and two racers, Brett Lunger and Arturo Merzario, unstrapped Niki and pulled him out. He walked several paces and then collapsed. Nurburgring officials broadcast that Niki Lauda had had a 'slight accident and was in no danger'. The accident, they reported, was due to 'mechanical failure of the car'. But then, as everyone knows, Nurburgring officials always blame every accident on 'mechanical failure', which for one hundred and thirty deaths, must be something of a record.

When he recovered consciousness Niki Lauda knew two things: one, that his face and lungs were burnt. Very badly burnt, fatally burnt most doctors agreed. The other thing Niki knew was that he was going to live. His optimism at this point was shared by no one, except his wife of six months, Marlene, who had started her vigil at his side. To stay alive for Niki was straightforward: he had to stay conscious. As long as he was conscious he was alive. His mind, in a way that is perhaps curious to most of us, ruled his body completely. Which is fortunate, for his body, by day three, was in a very bad way. A priest came in to give him the last rites.

'I was so cross you know, I wanted to say "Hey, stop this, this is the worst fuck up you make in your life. I am not going to die." ' He could not speak, so he lay in silent rage as the priest prayed, blessed and touched him.

'This is very bad, if I was a weak person and the priest comes in and gives me the last rites I would just give up. They should not do this, they should come and say "You are looking wonderful today", give you some encouragement.'

So Niki Lauda willed himself alive. If this sounds far-fetched or glib then the mistake is mine for putting it too simply. This is something you have to experience to know. I was in a bad crash once and when I first recovered consciousness I had no control of my body whatsoever. There was a high-pitched noise that I could not stop coming from somewhere in my chest, and there was blood leaking down from my head on to the rich brown earth making red patterns which were not altogether displeasing. Then I went into a huge and comforting blackness. When I recovered consciousness, I did not, like most bad literature tells us, think I was in heaven. I knew exactly where I was: still in the spot where I had thought I was going to die. Only now I could control my body. There were no strange sounds in my chest and I could raise my head, flex my fingers, wrist, arm and even move one leg. This was very good news – my spine was not broken. I was not paralysed. It was then that I knew I was not going to die. It took no great amount of will power to stay alive. I simply did not entertain the thought of death any more. What is more I'm in the *Lancet* to prove it. When you break too many bones, marrow gets released into your blood stream and you die from something called 'fat embolism'. I lived.

On a bigger and more conscious scale Niki Lauda willed himself alive.

'My lungs turned to shit, but I kept conscious and alive. In this I was helped by Marlene and the doctors who all gave me support. Marlene was fantastic. I mean she could have come in and gone completely hysterical. But she was strong and gave me strength. And now our love is even stronger.'

Marlene's view of herself is different.

'It was terrible, it is very difficult to describe . . . ' She pirouetted away from me, for reviving bad memories. Then she embarrassedly tried to communicate her distress. 'I could not show what I felt. I cannot now.' (This was before a race in America.) 'I am not very brave. But sometimes . . . '

After a decent interval of disinterest the news media suddenly realised that Niki Lauda, unbelievably, was alive. So they wanted to speak to him, which was impossible; in which case they wanted a picture of him, especially after he had undergone extensive skin grafting to his face.

'One day when the nurse went out and left the door unlocked a photographer came in and took my photograph. I could do nothing. I just lay there. But this is not right, to make money out of other people's misery.'

Marlene added, 'When we got out of hospital to our home in Austria, which is high up in the mountains and very isolated, we were surrounded by photographers and journalists all the time. We had to call the police to get them away.'

Almost unbelievably he raced again six weeks after his accident – in Italy, at Monza – and came fourth. Put that plainly it seems natural and easy. Crash – hospital – race again. But remember the nature of the crash, the nature of the massive injuries sustained, and the nature of this quite extraordinary young man. As one doctor put it, 'Unfortunately, as doctors, I do not think we can contribute a great deal, because of the very nature of Grand Prix accidents. Either they are minor or else there is massive trauma in which the vital structures cannot be salvaged and the outcome is fatal. There are freak cases where a highly qualified doctor can help, like Mark Donohue who suffered an epidural haematoma after his crash. A burst blood vessel in his brain. A neurosurgeon would have spotted that immediately and operated to relieve the pressure. As it was, no one recognised what was the matter until it was too late.'

And Lauda's accident? 'The man should by all accounts be dead.'

And here I was at another race track, in the pits with the press buzzing around him and the photographers clicking relentlessly.

'Get a shot of his ear,' I heard one pressman say to a photographer. The point is that Niki no longer has a left ear. His face goes into an angry, red-scarred vortex, that once was an ear. The flames took care of that. The only

14

concession Niki makes to vanity is that he wears a hat of some sort all the time. The fire took away most of one side of his scalp and hair as well. The people and press want to look at the man who survived and to ponder on what he looks like now.

His face will change, the red scars will soften, the new skin stretched too tight or spread too loosely will even out. The myriad small lumps on his face will disappear and further surgery will enable him to blink his one over-stretched eyelid. But where most people would hide their face, Niki does not.

Once I got to know him, it was only at a distance, strangely, that his face still shocked me, however slightly. Close up, his personality and what he was saying overrode totally the image of the scarred face.

So what is it that impels men like Niki Lauda? What is it that makes him and his fellow drivers, James Hunt, Jody Scheckter, Patrick Depailler, Emerson Fittipaldi and a host of others, put their lives on the line about once a month? They know the dangers, and in Niki's case he has defied both race and medical odds. Why do they do it, this curious thing called Formula One racing? A lot of it is tied up with the world championship. But let us begin at the beginning.

Formula One

The sport is still there, in winning the World Championship. Niki Lauda, Formula One World Champion, 1975.

The sport has gone out of it. I'm out now for winning and the money. James Hunt, Formula One World Champion, 1976.

Years ago we used, as a sport, to have gladiatorial combat. But like all good things, it was stopped; too bloody, people taking too much time off to see the ultimates (as the finals were known in those days); what to do with the one-eyed, one-armed, one-legged survivors? Besides which the benefit fights were unbelievably tedious. So they were ended. After a suitable interval we invented motor racing.

At the turn of the century people started racing across the countryside. From Paris mainly, which is why to this day the Fédération Internationale de l'Automobile, F.I.A., and its motor race governing subsidiary, Commission Sportive Internationale, C.S.I., is French based and the rule book, in *French*, takes precedence over all others. Theoretically this should end all arguments, but in practice it is the starting point of some truly epic disputes, involving race drivers, team managers, track officials, the public, the C.I.S., the F.I.A., noted French scholars, lexicographers and Uncle Tom Cobbley and all. There used to be races from

Paris to Marseilles and back, races from Paris to Berlin, and one memorable race from Paris to Madrid in which the carnage among racers and spectators reached such epic proportions that all races were banned for a while. The 'sport' of course was by all accounts prodigious, as always in direct proportion to the number of dead.

Cheating and chicanery did not start, as some would believe, with last year's races, but flourished from the start. It was not unknown for some wealthy young blood to start a race (all drivers had to be wealthy in those days), then head with his car and mechanic to the nearest discreet railway halt, where he, car and mechanic would embark on a train, make for the private coach where they would be joined by some *jeune fille*, who would entertain them for a few days before the racer and car were unloaded to flash across the winning line to the applause of the multitude and the ever-tiring, winning honours that were bestowed upon them.

There were, of course, also men who were totally devoted to motor racing. Since there was no sponsorship they paid their own way, buying the huge ungainly cars (which were eminently unsuited for going to market, let alone racing), modifying them, trying another model. It was an age in which racing can truly be said to have influenced and bettered car design. Everything was tried, wooden wheels, spoked wheels, different suspensions, front brakes! Mercedes used a large chain for its final drive to the rear wheel and only changed to the more conventional prop shaft when too many of their drivers were decapitated when the chain broke. There was a large, polyglot number of companies making cars and engines, some lasting for no more than their first and last model. But a surprising number are with us still. Fiat, Renault, Lancia, Mercedes. There is an old photograph of a young Enzo Ferrari driving a Lancia in a swirl of heat, excitement and dust, which explains a great deal of his present-day obsession with seeing that *his* Ferraris are the best race cars in the world.

At the cars grew bigger and faster, rules were imposed, mostly in an effort to curb the death rate among the spectators, who would wander lemming-like in front of the juggernauts, whose drivers, because of the dust on the roads, could barely make out the direction of travel, let alone whether there were obstacles in the way.

The First World War was regarded, if one is to believe the journals of the time, as a bloody nuisance between races. After World War One there was a change of emphasis in racing. The car manufacturers became interested. To sell cars you had to be seen to race, and to win. The racing cars resembled less and less the off-the-shelf tourer and the day of the sponsored driver began. To be sure, it still was a great help to have a lot of money or a title, or both, but now for the first time there was also a chance for the talented man in the street to race. Some of the races began to be run in circuits. There was of course a huge outcry. The circuits, manufacturers and paid drivers would be the death of motor-sport. Brooklands, now long dead as a circuit, because it became too dangerous, was known contemptuously by the road racers as the mill pond, 'Because you just went round and round the bloody thing,' as one old-timer told me.

Most races, as a consequence of a ban on open road racing in Britain, took place on the Continent. Then some highly innovative designers started turning out cars which were faster and better. There were Alfa-Romeos, the elegant Bugattis (Count Bugatti called the large racing Bentley, the British pride and joy, 'The fastest tractor on the road'), Maseratis, Talbots, Mercedes and Auto Union. Auto Union was a newcomer to racing but they made up for it by having a designer of genius, Dr Ferdinand Porsche, responsible later for the popular Volkswagen, the extremely fast Porsche and on the some-you-win-some-you-lose side, a tank, during World War Two, that happily for us, would not travel over 4 m.p.h. no matter what he did. At Auto Union Dr Porsche was helped by a driver of considerable ability, Adolph Rosenberger. Together they devised a rear-engined V-16 racer, which in 1934 was totally revolutionary. To get the polar moment of inertia of the car lower (i.e. to make it go around corners better, in ordinary English) they put the petrol tank behind the driver, who then looked very much like an appendage stuck on to a guided missile. Hitler took an interest in the amount of prestige that a win in Grand Prix racing brought to the country and gave both Auto Union and Mercedes liberal state aid. He also took an interest in the fact that Rosenberger was Jewish. He left the team and Germany ... But that is another book.

To drive their monster, Auto Union engaged an ex-motorcycle rider who had never driven racing cars before, which was probably just as well. Bernd Rosemeyer pronounced the car to be incomparable, the best and the fastest. Other drivers tried it and were horror-struck: it was totally unmanageable. This little scene was replayed some years later in 1972 in Britain. March Engineering had built a revolutionary racing car, the R721X, which they then gave to their team driver Ronnie Petersen. This car too had a 'low polar moment of inertia' and was designed by Robin Herd. He and Max Mosley, co-owners of March Engineering, were certain that this car was a world beater. Petersen tested the car and pronounced it magnificent. There was also a young driver on the team, who as Max Mosley admits, 'We didn't think much of. Inexperienced and in our opinion, didn't have the makings of a top class driver.'

This driver, who had bought his way into the team, i.e. he was paying to drive, not being paid, insisted that he too be given the new supercar. March Engineering obliged. He tested it and climbed out.

'The car is undriveable and very dangerous,' he said.

'Well,' said Max Mosley, 'here we had a world class driver telling us the car was fine, and some unknown telling us it was no good. Who do we believe? Petersen of course.'

Unfortunately, Petersen was totally wrong, and the then inexperienced, unknown driver, Niki Lauda, one hundred per cent correct. Niki is, as all designers and engineers and

19

mechanics who have worked with him tell you, 'Totally professional. He knows more about his car than any other driver on the track. This sometimes leads to problems . . . ' the latter said a little ruefully. The R721X was scrapped and a new car designed and made in nine weeks, which is some sort of record, even if the 'revolutionary car' was not. March Engineering certainly deserve another prize (the Wooden Wheel?) for having had two potential world champions (and one actual, Jackie Stewart) drive for them, and then wanting, or letting, them move on to other teams. James Hunt, the other ex-March driver, claims that they deliberately sabotaged his car at Monaco, in an effort to get him to break his contract and get out of the team. The reason they wanted the then impecunious James out, was that another driver with more charisma (i.e. money) wanted to join their team. After the race in the subnormal car, James Hunt and March Engineering exchanged words. Exit Hunt. This, of course, is James Hunt's side of the story and since all team managers are honourable men and all drivers notorious liars, with bad memories to boot, there is obviously some fault in the story.

Back to Auto Union and Mercedes. They refined their cars until the unbelievably beautiful Mercedes of 1937. It looks to an older generation a 'proper racing car'. Engine kicking out some 600 brake horse power (c.f. 500 b.h.p. for a modern Formula One), set in front of the driver. Body smooth and moulded, like a woman's breasts, not the aerodynamically sharp and aggressive shape we have today. Spoked wheels, with drum brakes, tyres recognisable as motorcar tyres. And no roll bars, safety harness or fire extinguishers cluttering up the line or the cockpit.

After World War Two the cars continued for a while much as before, but the emphasis was altering. Circuits were developed, then in 1950 the Grand Prix Formula One, as we know it today, started. In 1960 the racing cars were transformed virtually overnight. It was discovered that a rear-engined car could indeed go round corners very fast.

There were other changes in this period, disc brakes, vastly different tyres, lower cars and finally more and more aerodynamic shapes until finally scoops on the front to keep the wheels down and aerofoils on the rear wheel for traction. But the big car manufacturers were pulling out of racing as arguments developed about cost and the 'use of motor racing to motor manufacturing'. While the motor manufacturers dithered the rest of the advertising world jumped in and sponsorship began. With the exception of Ferrari, which still sticks rigidly to motor allied sponsorship, the cars were increasingly used as high speed bill-boards. Ronnie Petersen at one point was sponsored by some Chinese and his car was suitably inscribed with Chinese characters, none of which he, or his team, understood. It could have read, for all they knew, 'F1 racing is an imperialist paper tiger', as Max Mosley observed. We also have the 'First National City Bank Travellers Cheques Team Penske'. Swallow that, Linda Lovelace, if you can. There is also the 'Murchies Creameries Libre' which has, I am sure, been dreamed up by a cunning linguist. There are a host of cigarette sponsors and finally the car that the BBC feared more than Ken Tynan (he who finally said 'Fuck' on telly), the Surtees Durex. They banned motor racing from television because of this. It was pointed out that a great many more people have died from smoking than from fucking. But the BBC dug its corporate heels in. They refused first to transmit races with the Durex car in them, then when Durex obligingly blanked out their offensive name, they still refused. They were baulking at 'All that advertising on the cars, contrary to the BBC charter you know.' BBC spokesman. I spent an entertaining hour trying to explain what BBC policy was to an American. What it gets down to, of course, is not advertising, because in cricket, rugby and any other sport there is a great deal, but the fact that the head of sport loathes all motor and motorcycle racing. Departmental heads can be very powerful people in the BBC.

In motor racing, safety as well began to play a part after a disastrous crash in Le Mans in the 'fifties when over eighty spectators were killed.

'If a driver runs out of track or has a bad shunt and gets killed, well, that's all in the game. That's what he's paid for. If a man and his family who have come out for an afternoon's entertainment get killed, then that's a tragedy.' C.S.I. safety official.

Track safety was improved but it was and is a slow business. Lauda was particularly incensed on this point. 'For instance at Watkins Glen the Armco fence (a protective barrier) should have a standard bolt and a retaining washer. The safety committee of the drivers said that washers must be fitted on all bolts to hold the steel fence more securely. So they do nothing and a driver, Koenig, hits the fence at 30 m.p.h. and the bottom guard rail breaks away, his car goes underneath, and he was decapitated by the top rail. Do you know they have now installed retaining washers in two per cent of the bolts? They will get 100,000 paying spectators. A lot of money and they will do nothing. If I don't race because I think the track is unsafe then I am a shit and all the people say "Those drivers are bastards." And if we race and someone gets killed then they say "Those drivers are so stupid, why do they race!" '

The race cars have now reached the point in development where the difference in speed and power in virtually all cars starting a race will be small. Their reliability, road holding and their driver's ability will not, which is what makes for winners and losers. Twice world champion Emerson Fittipaldi is a good example of this. He changed cars for a 'Copersucar', sponsored by a sugar firm, which has proved to be unreliable and a touch slower than the McLarens and the Lotus's that he drove formerly. Fittipaldi is now nowhere in the world championship. Another sidelight on the unfortunate Mr Fittipaldi's career is that every track announcer anglicises the name of his car and announces it as the 'Coppersucker' which when said fast enough comes out as 'cocksucker'. Not a well-bred name, or car.

Fittipaldi's name comes near the end of the list of Formula One Grand Prix Champions, since 1950. They are an international lot: Guiseppe Farina (Italy), Juan Fangio (Argentina), Alberto Ascari (Italy), Mike Hawthorn (England), Jack Brabham (Australia), Phil Hill (U.S.A.), Graham Hill (England), Jim Clark (Scotland), John Surtees (England), Denis Hulme (New Zealand), Jackie Stewart (Scotland), Jochen Rindt (Austria), Emerson Fittipaldi (Brazil), Niki Lauda (Austria) and James Hunt (England). Some of course have won the championship more than once, Juan Fangio an incredible five times. But, sadly, the names of the champions are in a way a litany of the quick and the dead. Farina, killed testing; Ascari, killed testing; Hawthorn, killed in his very fast Jaguar; Clark, killed racing; Graham Hill killed, Rindt killed in practice.

It is a hard cruel sport, but one in which the rewards now are commensurate with the risks. The chances of survival of an F1 driver are approximately one in thirteen, but a world champion can now expect to retire a millionaire after a few seasons' racing.

The top drivers all know that their chosen profession is extremely dangerous.

'Of course Formula One racing is dangerous. Any driver who does not think so is a fool.' Niki Lauda. Then he added, 'When there is a death from racing it moves me but does not throw me off balance because you know that it is to be expected in this business. I don't worry about it, this is will power. I recognise the risks but I do not worry about them. This would affect my judgement in races adversely.'

Part of the inescapable danger is now built into the nature of racing. The rear-engined cars remove one large barrier which the old drivers had between them and oblivion, in any head-on confrontation. The engine, as it ripped itself to pieces, would absorb some of the energy of impact. Given time, a modern race driver will deliberately swing his car around and slam backwards into danger, using the engine as a cushion. The critical element is time. There is not always time for the slow slew around. The cars are low and they travel fast. A good driver will be on the limit all the time. This is what makes a good driver. If something, often an infinitesimal change in adhesion, suspension, anything, pushes him over the limit, he is in trouble. Another problem is that on modern circuits the places where you can pass another car are limited. With two experienced drivers pushing their cars hard, passing becomes extremely difficult. On one corner the one car may not have enough acceleration, on another, not enough adhesion. In the old days, despite what they say, it was easier in this respect. The cars were large but higher and narrower, and all drivers would use what is known as the slingshot effect. You tuck yourself in behind the man in front of you, trust him absolutely (for if he brakes suddenly at a hundred and fifty miles per hour you are both in for a surprise) and then wait for where you want to overtake him. His car clears a path of air and you are literally towed along in the vacuum he is creating just behind his car. You ease off on the accelerator because of this. Now! Give it the heavy boot, out and past. Wish me luck as you wave me good-bye.

Today's F1 cars present a problem. They are designed to cut through the air with a minimum drag, thus for the slingshot effect to operate, you have to get very close indeed. There is also another problem. The wedge-shaped racers have carefully designed aerofoils front and rear of the body, designed to increase roadholding. Both aerofoils depend on a smooth flow of air passing over them to give maximum down thrust. When you come up close to another F1 car, at high speed, the front aerofoil gets into the turbulent airstream of the lead car. *In a high speed corner* the steering and roadholding capability of the following car will be severly diminished. Enough virtually to guarantee a shunt. So the slingshot effect is used very judiciously, below certain speeds.

I watched Hunt and Sheckter battling it out in a race. Sheckter in front. Hunt with balletic precision glued himself for a few seconds just a yard behind Sheckter's car. They approached the chicane, which Sheckter had been asked to design, to slow the racers down. In on the same line, as though indissolubly linked together, and then with a flick and a roar Hunt was past him. He did it so well he made it look easy. It is a deceptive ease. There are a number of things that a top driver will do or use which the casual observer will not notice at all. Lauda will on occasion apparently hit the kerbing. When you see him do this it is as well to remember that he is probably one of the most precise drivers in the world today. He hits the kerb because he has deliberately aimed one rear wheel at it; this throws his car off and back into a corner much faster than it would under normal conditions. Watch for this little trick particularly when he is putting in a high speed practice lap.

Generally, as in all high definition sports, i.e. those very fast and very dangerous, it takes a practised eye to spot the differences in styles between competitors. Quite often driving style is dictated by the car. Lauda, given the time, can adjust his suspension for a particular track so precisely that he does not have to use a great deal of physical effort to drive the car. Hunt relishes the battle with his car and he drives it with an animal zest. Sheckter is temperamental, blowing hot and then cold in his driving. There are of course the more obvious sideshows, Brambilla crashing before, during and unbelievably after, winning a race. But not Lauda. His line is unaltered because he is driving on the limit and he knows the limit precisely.

He has other problems now however. Under certain conditions, because of his accident, 'the brake will come on in my brain'. The mind, that curious repository of fact, fiction and ambiguity, has in Lauda's case stored one fact that he does not consciously know himself. That is the fact of how and why he crashed at Nurburgring. When certain of those

25

conditions are duplicated on the track Lauda cannot and will not race.

Another of Niki's problems, one which he shares with all racers, is that the cars have to be raced and tuned constantly to keep them perfect. His accident not only stopped this constant process, but to a certain extent had a knock-on effect, on to the next season. The machines have become almost human in the amount of attention they need.

III

The Machines

You must know a lot about engines. Author.

A lot is a big word, a little is better. Dr Mauro
Forghieri, Chief Design Engineer, Ferrari Racing.

Once it could be said that all F1 cars and motor cars had in
common was four wheels. Now even that is not true; the
Tyrrells have six wheels.

Formula One racing cars are the ultimate in what is
apparently a contradiction. They are custom-made utility
cars. They cost about £40,000, basic, if you can get someone to sell you one. All cars have a maximum capacity of
three litres: the rule book says so. The rule book also
decrees how wide they will be, how high they will be, their
minimum width, where and how the aerofoil will be affixed
and a host of other things.

Because designers are inventive the rule book is constantly being modified and added to. You cannot simply
sit down and design an F1 racer as the fancy takes you.
There are stringent if somewhat obscure regulations (rule
book) and parameters (mainly tyres) governing all phases
of design and construction.

I saw my first Formula One racer in the window of Heal's
department store. It is a good place to study a tough un-
compromising car, surrounded by the detritus of the con-
sumer society. The cars are built to do one thing only, go

as fast as possible around a number of different tracks and win. I have no idea what Heal's was built for.

The racers look, from a distance, like low, brightly coloured wedges with sharp edges in unexpected places. They have air scoops in various places, ducting the air over radiators which cool engine water, oil and gearbox oil. Ducts also force cool air over the brakes. There is always an aerofoil over the rear axle and in the front usually a long protruding scoop aerofoil to keep the front wheels down or sometimes some aerodynamic shape designed to lessen front wheel wind resistance.

The development of aerofoils has had a significant effect on the design of all race cars. The aerofoil as it cuts through the air acts the opposite way to an aircraft wing. Instead of lifting, it pushes down on the wheel. Aerofoils are also effective only above certain speeds, determined by design and the angle which they bite into the wind. With a lot of wing the car will have high downthrust, hence adhesion on corners, but will also be less capable of high speed on the straights because of the drag effect as it goes through the air. So always the aerofoil angle is a compromise adjusted continually in practice laps to get the best effect. Also, because the art of aerofoil design is in its infancy, shapes come and go every season. To begin with the rear aerofoils were fixed high above the car by two struts (to avoid air turbulence and thus be more efficient). Unfortunately these struts had a habit of breaking off just when the aerofoil was most needed, with disastrous results. Nowadays aerofoil height, width, fixing and size are strictly governed by the C.S.I.

The body shell of an F1 racer, as distinct from the old racers is a fragile structure, usually lightweight plastic which can be removed with four screws. Below this body, designed for aerodynamic effect, is the car proper. The odd thing about F1 cars is that, to save weight, they are very fragile; you cannot lean or sit wherever you wish. An inlet will twist off, or a radiator will come out of true. The main

28

body of the car is a steel monocoque shell which doubles as the petrol tank. Very roughly an oval doughnut, the hole in the middle for the driver to sit in. This shell is lined on the inside with rubber, to prevent petrol leaks, and is filled with expanded polystyrene, which means that the foamy plastic occupies a large volume and is very light and porous. The petrol does not slosh around in this honeycomb structure, which is useful when you are cornering and it leaks out more slowly if it breaks, which is very useful in a fire.

On to this petrol tank-cum-body are bolted the front wheels, steering and suspension, the rear wheels, suspension, engine, gear box and differential. The front wheels are small, wide and have a flat treadless surface for racing in the dry. The rear wheels are the same except that they are enormous. And very expensive. There is also a set of tyres with treads for racing in the wet. There was once a proliferation of tyres from various manufacturers but for one reason or another they dropped out. Now there is only Goodyear. At a track depending on the surface and conditions, the Goodyear man will announce that there are such and such tyres available. Wet and dry. The choice of tyre is limited to different mixes of polymers in the tyre, which give different characteristics of adhesion and hardness. These tyres, when inflated, do not bulge on the surface that touches the road, unlike ordinary tyres. On the contrary, due to some extraordinary engineering the surface in contact with the track actually becomes more and more level as it is blown up.

This restriction in availability of tyres has had a consequence on car design. Once the designers could dream up exotic configurations of body and suspension and then ask an obliging firm, say 'Simon Hyman Indestructible Tyres' to build them a set of tyres that were of such-and-such a profile inflated and with a special softness and adhesion. Simon Hyman could then stick the company's name on one side of the car, not too near the cockpit, please, and a bit

29

smaller because of the BBC and scatology. Now the cars, on all designers' admission, are designed around the tyres, and of course the rule book.

The rule book, as mentioned, is put out by the F.I.A. and C.S.I. in French (with an English translation). A designer: 'The book designs the car, some of the rules are for safety, but some are trivial. Because of cross-referencing you will find the specification for a particular material used in construction for *all* cars is in, say, the saloon production car section. It's terrible. Only the French could dream up something so totally logical and so totally confusing. It's also a bad read.'

This fact was graphically confirmed at Monza (see page 59) where the rule book was so confusing on petrol octane numbers (octane number roughly equals kick) that the race organisers telegrammed the C.S.I. for clarification of their totally ungrammatical and jargon-filled text. The C.S.I. cabled back: 'The rule is as interpreted by the rule book.' Ah, yes, well . . .

Most cars have five forward gears with one reverse and are tailor-made to fit one driver. The driver's space is limited; he will have a seat moulded exactly to his body shape, inside the monocoque chassis-cum-petrol tank, and all levers and pedals will be placed exactly where *he* feels comfortable with them. The three litre engine has about five times as much power as the ordinary saloon car and is somewhat different to drive. James Hunt: 'The clutch is a bit fierce and you have to keep the engine running fast, not idling. The sensation is very difficult to describe. It's totally different from driving an ordinary car in that a racing car is totally functional, no bullshit on it. And it is fast, really fast, like you can't imagine until you try it. But you do get used to it after a while. The forces are enormous. In an ordinary car you'd be covered in bruises, that's why you need the tailor-made seat. When you start you mustn't slip the clutch too much or else with all that power going through it you'll burn it out. That's the problem with starts. You

30

should slip the clutch and not get too much wheel spin because that loses you traction and speed. Ideally you want to use your clutch and get the power gently but then you burn out your clutch and make a super start for twenty yards, and you walk back to the pits. That's why I make bad starts. I must work on it.'

The clutch has brass, not asbestos, insets for toughness. Niki Lauda smiled faintly when asked about his starts.

'Every time James Hunt and I are together, I beat him on the start.'

Inside the driver's seat, in contrast to the glittering emblazoned exteriors, all is drab. Besides clutch, accelerator and brake, there is a rev counter, to give engine speed, an oil pressure gauge (indicating the oil supply to the engine), an oil temperature gauge, a fuel gauge, a water temperature gauge, a start button and a tiny steering wheel. On the Ferrari the engine rev counter registers from 4,000 r.p.m. to 14,000 r.p.m. This and the oil pressure gauges are very important. When your oil pressure drops below 8-9 kg/sq cm then you have problems.

'You don't get much time to watch the gauges. When you are racing hard you are too busy concentrating on the race. It is only when you are ahead that you start watching the gauges. Even then if something goes wrong there is nothing much you can do about it.' Niki.

In the Monaco Grand Prix, a race Niki won, his oil pressure dropped to virtually zero on the last few laps. 'Another lap and I was finished.'

As we need air, cars need oil. The Ferrari also has a limiter built into the ignition system. This is designed to cut the engine out progressively if a gear is missed and it is overrevved, something which even Niki can do. There is a switch to change petrol pumps from electrical to mechanical. The electrical pump works more efficiently at very low engine revs, then it is switched over to the mechanical pump. The main reason for this is that in case of an accident, the petrol flow will stop as the engine stops. Similarly there is an emergency switch to stop all electricity. There are usually two fire extinguishers, one for the driver, one for the engine, and a small life support tube which the driver clips on to his helmet. This gives him a direct feed of air in time of emergency. The fire extinguisher 'only gives about a ninety second blast. We reckon it's better to try to put it all out at once. If this doesn't work, well then nothing much else we can install in the car will make much difference.' The big extinguishers must come from trackside. Because of weight considerations the front and sides of the car cannot be strengthened like some family saloons to crumple progressively and absorb impact in an accident. The driver is always very vulnerable. There is also a considerable physical effort involved in racing. Niki Lauda, physically small, and to look at not a man of great physical strength, lets the car do the work for him. 'I am not strong, but I am strong enough.'

Even so, after a race it takes him a couple of days to relax mentally and physically. James Hunt: 'I used to play county squash and only once can I remember the all pervasive exhaustion that I get after every Grand Prix race.'

Most racers agreed the Monaco was the most demanding and exhausting track, 'Because there is no place to relax. You are cornering, accelerating, changing gear, braking, doing something all the time.' Niki. Jackie Stewart dissented. 'There is one place where I relax on the Monaco track, it helps a great deal.' He then went on to explain that he relaxed his neck for precisely .4 of a second at a certain point between gear changes.

An interesting indication of different racing styles can be seen in the hands of Lauda and Hunt. Lauda's are small, light-boned, precise and smooth. Hunt's are large, muscular and with the hard callouses of an old-time blacksmith.

How then are these cars designed for men who will drive them on the limit all the time? There are a number of ways. You can start from scratch, recruit a designer, Dr Harvey Postlethwaite, a team manager, 'Bubbles' Horsley, a driver,

Hunt the Shunt, call yourself Le Patron, spend half a million pounds and have precisely nothing to show for it at the end of the day, except a reputation for being terribly British, or rather silly, depending on one's point of view. That is the story of Hesketh racing. There are other ways. Sometimes when you do not have much money you have to use talent instead. The engine that most racing cars use today is a good example of this, the Ford-Cosworth. These engines will set you back about £15,000 each. Most teams have a minimum of one spare engine and usually enough spares to build one more engine at a pinch.

Keith Duckworth was mainly responsible for the Ford-Cosworth design with some money from Ford. The team consisted of Duckworth, one chief designer, three design draughtsmen and one development engineer. This team was based on the principle of six people equals six ideas. The main problem with this engine which is a V-8, was that it tended to blow up with monotonous regularity, leaving oil on the track and egg on everyone's faces. Resonance was the problem; to put it simply, the engine had a habit of shaking itself to bits. Designer Alan Walters: 'To begin with we tried increasing the moments of inertia of the gears, then we put a toothed disc on the crankshaft and measured the time interval on the disc to get a beat frequency. Above nine-five we were getting a very complicated response. Keith Duckworth removed one bearing support and allowed the shafts to cantilever, he extended the shafts through the front cover and fitted a displacement translator on the shafts and the problem began to resolve into component parts. Eventually we used a torsion bar with two degrees of freedom on the idler gears. This worked.'

Bertrand Russell once remarked that the only reason that he was able to write in extremely simple and lucid English was that he had proved to his critics that he could be highly obscure, in *Principia Mathematica*, a tome of quite remarkable density. What the designer is saying is that they tried making the gears stronger by making them heavier. This

3   33

did not work so they observed the precise speed at which the engine started to shake itself to pieces. A measurement on the amount of movement on each of the rods supporting the gears was made. More flexible rods on two of the gears stopped the trouble.

One of the problems in building racing cars and engines is that it is easy to build an engine with the same performance as everyone else; it is getting reliability and a small gain in power between one and two per cent which is difficult. Cosworth have now come out with a new engine, lighter and with higher power, close to 500 b.h.p. Every part in the engine is designed to take a certain maximum load. If it can take more it is overweight and must be trimmed down. The extra power of the engine now poses a whole host of related problems.

The con rods were designed to take a certain stress. Ditto the crankshaft bearings and the gear box. In the middle of an interview James Hunt saw one of the Cosworth design team. Instantly he was all business.

'The new engine?' asked Hunt.

'Down on weight, up on power.'

'That's good, what's the reliability like?' Earnestly.

The engineer was silent for a while. 'We'll just have to suck it and see.'

A glum pall descended on the conversation.

One of the most common causes of engine failure is when a driver misses a gear and puts his foot down hard. The engine responds immediately, overrevving, and can blow itself up or overstrain one component, which will soon fail. The limiter on the Ferrari goes some way, but not all, to curing this. There is nothing the designer can do about an engine blow-up except curse the driver, silently or loudly, because whatever any of them say ('I am not involved in the people, the sport, the money, the politics, I am only involved in the technical side.' Mauro Forghieri), they do get deeply emotionally involved in their engines. Alan Walters, March Engineering: 'The great thing in motor

34

racing is to stay detached, because if you don't you make the wrong decision. Some drivers drive you mad but you must not lose your cool, you have to think of the problem in a rational manner and then do something. It's no use simply doing something because the driver says it's the thing to do. They are invariably wrong. Also I hate major changes at the circuits, they never work.'

Why then did he come to the race track? 'You should be with the team at a race to know what is happening – also you keep an eye on everyone else to see that they are not stealing a march on you.'

In a small firm the designer will be called on to do a bit of everything, not always with happy results. One designer was asked to design a new aerofoil for a racer. He got out the relevant books, read all there was to read, then picked his shape. This was duly tested in the wind tunnel and then pronounced fine. The car was tested and the driver was enthusiastic. But could he have a little more downthrust, and more and more . . . ? The designer knew at this point that there was something definitely wrong because theoretically the driver was getting more downthrust on his rear wheels than he needed, yet he was asking for more. The rear wheel was now breaking away terrifyingly in high speed corners. Then fortunately the designer realised what was wrong. When the car went into a corner the flow of air across the wing was changing from head-on to side-on. The side-on air-flow pattern on the wing had never been tested. At an oblique angle the downthrust capability of the aerofoil altered dramatically, hence the rear wheels suddenly sliding as the high force acting down on them became negligible. 'I was so proud of my first aerofoil and I suppose the driver didn't want to upset me by telling me it was a bummer. Fortunately we found out what was wrong before anything drastic happened.' This is how drivers get killed testing.

To Jody Scheckter designers were definitely bad news: 'You know I can talk to anybody – mechanics, fans, race officials, everyone – except designers. They're something else. Look at this bloody thing.' He banged the large support on his car's aerofoil disparagingly.

There is a different atmosphere at Ferrari and with Niki Lauda. First of all, Ferrari *is* Enzo Ferrari, and the great, gleaming red F1 monster is his child, now his only and best beloved. It is his life's work, ambition and dream. He and the machine are inseparable, to slight the motor is to insult the maker.

'The Ferrari from which a wheel breaks does not exist. If anyone says once more that Lauda crashed because of mechanical failure in my car, I will withdraw Ferrari totally from world racing.'

Mechanical failure in Niki's Ferrari has now become a taboo subject. The standards at Ferrari are high, some would say impossibly high. To look into the Ferrari works is not to discover a warm Italian factory, with everyone singing Rigoletto and drinking Chianti, rather it is an efficiency expert's dream. Mistakes are not tolerated and there is no let up in the demand for one hundred per cent perfection. Perfection also encompasses one prime point – winning. If you do not win at *everything* Ferrari enters then it is best to start consulting the situations vacant column, immediately. The man in charge of this is nearly eighty, either Commendatore or Cavaliere, Enzo Ferrari, Dot. Ing. Honoris Causei. He started out in life as the son of a metal worker (and some will say ended it as a son of something different) with no money, no titles, only a talent for and obsession with fast cars. The cars he helped design and race have changed over the years as they became faster and more lethal. Just before World War Two he left the Alfa-Romeo racing team and set up Scuderia Ferrari, not building his own cars but adapting existing designs. After 1945 he started building his own cars and the prancing black horse of Modena became known throughout the world. Ferrari had a son destined to follow in his father's footsteps, but he died aged twenty-three and his father returned from domesticity to dominate the business.

36

Lest any reader with £24,000 to spare at this point decides he wishes to own one of the top hand-made Ferrari sports cars (the 512 Berlinetta-Boxer) and perhaps outdrag the man next door in his Lamborghini, forget it. Enzo Ferrari has a habit of vetting people who buy his most expensive car. Just lately a call was put through to the factory – could a dealer take delivery of such a car for a star, internationally known, waiting cash in hand? No reply. Frantic telephone calls from the dealer, finally a no. Why? asked the hysterical dealer. Back came the laconic reply, Enzo Ferrari was of the opinion that the man would not be able to drive the car correctly. No sale.

Ferrari is now a subsidiary of the Fiat works but a condition of sale was that Enzo Ferrari kept control of the Ferrari factory and in particular the racing cars and effort. This arrangement suits both Fiat and Ferrari. Ferrari now has the backing and support of one of the largest motor car manufacturers in the world (with an assembly line in Russia) and Fiat, under Count Agnelli, in return enjoys the reflected glory and technological spin-offs from Ferrari. Before selling to Fiat, Ferrari was approached by Ford, who were looking for precisely this, in a European car manufacturer. Their terms were more than generous. Enzo Ferrari would have control of the factory, more than adequate research facilities and so on. There was one minor clause way down in the contract, Ford would control the race cars. That was the hole in the bucket, dear Henry, dear Henry, whereout leaked the entire agreement. At present the entire sports budget of Ferrari goes into Formula One racing. Results are obligatory. Mauro Forghieri, probably one of the world's top designers, went through a bad patch in the late sixties. His designs were not winning. He vanished into an obscure department to contemplate the mechanical equivalent of his navel.

'It is difficult to be close to a big man, a man who represents something important in the world. I am not small but I have found a way to work with him.' Mauro Forghieri.

It was only when he came up with the design of the 312 that he was reinstated. Harsh or near-sighted judgement? Perhaps, but then remember that if a world champion does not drive the Ferraris as Enzo Ferrari thinks they can and should be driven, then he too is either demoted or fired. John Surtees, 1964 World F1 champion, left because he did not keep winning. Niki Lauda did not compete in the Japanese Grand Prix. In his estimation it was a totally unnecessary risk. Enzo Ferrari thought differently, his cars had been let down and even though he still took the F1 constructors' cup on points he was hugely displeased with Niki. World Champion Niki Lauda was relegated to number two driver in the Ferrari team. He did not stay there long. Had he learnt that Ferrari is worth more than his life?

Niki has on occasion driven even when he has calculated that the odds were against him. In Barcelona in 1975, the track was dismally unsafe. The drivers organised a boycott, they were pressurised by the constructors to race, big money was at stake and they caved in. On a visibly dangerous circuit Niki went out and put in the fastest practice lap. His girl friend at the time, Mariella, was furious: 'You risked your life foolishly,' she berated him publicly. A sheepish Niki agreed, but now after one world championship and Nurburgring, his priorities have altered.

Enzo Ferrari, for all his obsessional regard for his race machines, is now, oddly enough, only seen at one race track in the world – Monza – and then only at practice. But despite, or probably because of, this he knows exactly how the team are shaping up. Conditions of the track, car, driver, practice times and any mistakes are all constantly telephoned through to him. He will have the final say as to whether a driver races or not. Here he is at variance with Niki.

'It is my business, my life, I am the judge whether I race or not.'

Hence the Japanese Grand Prix and the problems it caused. In *Brave New World* they prayed to Ford; in Modena they pray to Ferrari.

'You see drivers come to Ferrari not because we can guarantee them to win, but because we can guarantee to offer them the best of ourselves. We are more than a team, we have something which no others have . . .' Mauro Forghieri.

The Italian crowds at a track share in this something a great deal more than other nations. Niki: 'Well, it's always difficult driving for Italians. They are more emotionally involved with their car, their team. They expect more from you as a driver. But always *I* am the one who demands more from myself than anyone . . . Italians, Americans, anyone. In Monaco in 1975 the pressure for me to win was fantastic. Ferrari had not won there for twenty years. To begin with it was a battle for pole position. Finally I went out and did one lap and I knew I could not go faster. Fortunately it was the fastest. It is a difficult race but I put pressure on *myself* and won.'

Dr Mauro Forghieri is ultimately responsible for the design of the Ferrari 312T2, Niki's car. 'Three for three litre capacity, twelve for twelve horizontally opposed cylinders, T for transverse gearbox and two because it is the second model. Next year it is three.'

The Ferrari has the edge on all other engines in power, five hundred horsepower versus four hundred and sixty-five, almost precisely one per cent more power ('What you are looking for is a one per cent difference . . .').

'Niki has a power advantage over the rest of us which most drivers would not be able to exploit. He does and it makes him hard to beat.' James Hunt.

That Hunt beats Lauda speaks volumes for his ability. 'I have to push it hard – very.'

'Forghieri is responsible for a considerable engineering feat. Theoretically a twelve-cylinder car is more powerful than an eight-cylinder, like the Cosworth. But then you have friction losses which are much higher and lower reliability, because with more things to go wrong, they can and do. He is a very good engineer and has disproved sod's law, the one that says that if something can go wrong it will. Seriously though, he is good and his engine is better than any other.' Designer.

Here the rival designer's eyes lit up. 'He also has one of the best back-up facilities in the world. The whole Fiat empire.' I could almost see the engines he would love to build reflected in his eyes.

'I am allowed to do anything I want at Ferrari,' said Forghieri, 'of course I cannot, how you say, be silly, then I am no longer chief designer.' For silly read lose.

Forghieri joined Ferrari after his doctorate. He tried to join that well-known mirror of capitalism, the charitable organisation, Lockheed, but could not get a work permit, so he joined Ferrari. He has been involved in designing twenty-five engines, twelve gearboxes, twenty-five different types of car, sports cars, G.T. cars, F1, F2. (He drives a Lancia. There is a joke at the Ferrari factory that even Commendatore Enzo Ferrari cannot afford to drive a Ferrari.) He has designed six four-cylinder cars and eight twelve-cylinder cars, including Lauda's current car. He has also designed bodywork and aerofoils. He is very much a re-search and development man and insists, 'We go to make technical developments, not only to race. We are *not* part of the theatre.'

There is a considerable time lag in designing, testing, perfecting and racing an engine or car. Ferrari went through a long period (fifteen years) when they did not do at all well out of racing. Only now are the fruits of Forghieri's designs ripening. He comes to the race track only when it is vitally necessary, since he has a large team of technical assistants to cover the day-to-day exigencies of racing. Niki's accident necessitated a new car, which meant more work late in the season – then he was in constant attendance, listening to the impassive Niki, smiling broadly when he was right or as the car came successively into tune. Racers come and go but good designers go on for a long, long time.

During one race I listened to all the racers flashing past.

When they had to slow down for a sharp corner a lot of them missed beats and backfired. The two Ferraris alone were conspicuous in never missing a beat, I remembered.

'We cannot guarantee them to win . . . But we can guarantee to offer them the best of ourselves.'

IV

The Mechanics

You share the hard times and the champagne. Ermanno
Coughi, chief mechanic, Ferrari.

A racing team viewed from the outside consists mainly of
one glamorous entity. The superstar, the driver – Jackie
Stewart, James Hunt, Niki Lauda – then perhaps the technical nuts, the designers, then the team manager, the
speed groupies, pit helpers, then, low on the totem pole, the
mechanics. This is odd because it is primarily the mechanics
who liaise with the driver on the state of tune of his car and
hence running in the race on the day. These men are every
bit as skilled as the driver. To call them mechanics is a mis-
nomer; they are the high priests of the machine. They are a
breed apart from all other mechanics. The common or gar-
den mechanic has certainly had an underprivileged upbringing, a misunderstood childhood, done badly at school and
Borstal. The only way to get adequate revenge on society
was to join a garage, where these lovable rascals, up and
down the country, now 'fix' your car and mine.

I once had a perfectly reasonable Sunbeam Alpine which
I took in to the main dealer in Leeds for repair to one door
and for servicing. The car was, on its return, a juddering
wreck. The sound insulating material on the door was removed and not replaced; the window needed two hands to
raise and lower; the starter motor for some reason now
worked fifty per cent of the time. A jet was left out of one

of the carburettors. The engine suddenly lost water at an alarming rate through some never located hole. I tried to sell the car. The first prospective buyer was sceptical when the car would not start and listened appreciatively to the tinny slam of the repaired door. I tried my best hail-fellow-well-met attitude and said as I wound up one window, 'Well, the windows are perfect.' At this point the window dropped out and crashed to a thousand pieces in the road. The prospective buyer left hurriedly, no doubt thinking himself the victim of a macabre practical joke. A friend of mine patched the car up in the end, with suitable comments on the mechanics who had seemingly repaired it with deft touches of a sledge hammer.

It *must* have been different in the good old days. One merely has to look at the 1928 Rolls-Royce handbook, written for the owner's driver/mechanic. This is a thick tome and tells the gentleman's mechanic how to repair everything that might conceivably go wrong. And I mean everything. A considerable degree of skill and intelligence was obviously called for. At the end of the manual the owner was invited to send his driver/mechanic to the Rolls-Royce depot in North London on a course of further instruction. As well as this ' . . . an owner can arrange private lessons for himself should he so desire. This is for gentlemen who require tuition in the science of motor maintenance.' I like the use of the phrase 'science of motor maintenance'. Science, not art.

Besides the large band of misfits and rip-off artists masquerading as mechanics there is a small band of men who in some way are able to communicate with machines. They fall into two distinct groups. The one group are people who can resuscitate an engine when all others have failed. It will not go fast but it will go. In this operation they generally use a hairpin, some sticking plaster and half a potato. The other group are perfectionists, they will take an old engine and lovingly polish, rebore, refit, reroute oil feeds – 'The old Aston never really had an adequate supply of oil to the lower quadrant of the third big end' – and generally work on an engine until it is better than the designers intended.

I knew an Italian mechanic who got his hands on an ancient straight sixteen-cylinder Sunbeam-Talbot that Sir Henry Seagrave blew up in an attempt to set a world land-speed record. This mechanic lopped off the offending broken eight cylinders and rebuilt the remaining eight cylinders as a highly efficient new engine. This is a feat roughly comparable with splitting a human being down the middle and getting one half to function satisfactorily as a one-armed, one-legged person. I once shared a house with a good mechanic. He stripped an old Allard and then re-assembled it lovingly in the lounge. It was truly a wonderful sight, made more so by the wall we had to knock down to get the bloody car out.

Racing mechanics are a totally dedicated band. I watched a team of mechanics battling to get Fittipaldi's Copersucar into racing trim at eleven o'clock one night. A box approximating to Fittipaldi's weight was on the driver's seat as they worked without the usual banter. I went to bed. At seven the next morning in the otherwise deserted workshop they were still at it, grey with fatigue but still able to crack one joke.

'You lot are up early.' 'No, just late in going to bed.'

The life is not glamorous. All they generally see is an airport, a motel, and a race circuit. Towards the end of a season one race track tends to blur into another as the fatigue piles on. But even through the fatigue they will still retain the precision and deftness with their hands that their job demands. Because of the complexity of a modern racing car, virtually every nut and bolt has its own separate spanner of exactly the right length and angle for unscrewing and tightening. Working on a race engine is not like working on a saloon car. Although all mechanics can, they will rarely strip and rebuild an engine. Time and economics are against this. Instead they will simply install a new engine. 'In half an hour when time is very short.' Coughi.

The life of a race engine is approximately three races

before it needs to be completely overhauled, usually at the factory of origin, either Ferrari, Alfa, Matra or Cosworth. But before a race there is a veritable jungle of alterations and repairs to be made even if the car has not been in a shunt. If it has, there is even more work.

The cars and mechanics will generally arrive ahead of the drivers. The cars are uncrated and the work area set up. If the car finished in the last race a number of bits and pieces need replacing. Four new wheels – this is the easiest and can be done in fourteen or so seconds if the mechanics really get their skates on. Then there is a new clutch, new drive shafts, universal joints and brake pads. Then there will be a session with the driver rectifying any mechanical problems which have developed. Gear change stiff, one wheel braking harder than the other, engine not getting to peak revs, engine misfiring, some vague indefinable rattle in the nether regions. All will be attended to. Then comes the gearing. The mechanical configuration on an F1 car is, engine, drive shaft, differential, half-shaft and wheels, then gear-box. Unlike most saloon cars, which is engine, gear-box, drive shaft, etc. What this means is that the mechanics can get at the clutch and gear-box very quickly. Because every track is different, new gear ratios will be needed. The gearing that won in Monaco will be disastrous at Brands. Here the mechanics liaise very closely with the driver. The gearing must be exactly right for every corner, gradient, chicane and straight. Then comes the real mechanical hurdle. Once the engine and all related mechanical pieces are banging, pushing and whirling satisfactorily the chassis must be 'tuned' to the circuit. This may sound odd since it was once only the motor which had to be tuned and the rest followed. With today's high speed monster it is not enough to have a perfectly tuned engine. If the roadholding of the car is not in harmony with the circuit (and all circuits present a different challenge) then the race is lost before starting.

Now the mechanics really set to. Usually there will be three per car, each with definite functions. A formula must be quickly arrived at which pleases the driver (sometimes impossible), and makes for a fast reliable car.

'Those bastards are deliberately sabotaging my car. I told them it was something serious and they wouldn't listen to me.' Brett Lunger, after coasting to a halt during practice. This is unthinkable on any terms in the Ferrari team. Any suggestion that any of the ten mechanics on the team (as opposed to the usual seven) was doing anything less than a thousand per cent more than any comparable mechanic would probably trigger off World War Three. They modestly claim the best cars, the best drivers and the best mechanics. But the Ferrari team is undoubtedly formidable. One merely has to watch them set up shop at a race to confirm this. Besides the mechanics there are technicians who bustle about with statistics, slide rules and graphs, never smiling, occasionally mumbling something to a mechanic. Then there is a huge staff at the pits – time keepers, publicists, people with wheels, spanners, microphones, cameras, thermos flasks, bits of paper, bits of car, all bustling around like bees in a hive. It would be an interesting exercise to walk into this crowd and shout the Italian equivalent of 'Fuck Ferrari'.

Ferrari have more people, more spare engines, more spare parts, more crates than any other team. They also are the only team who mount a guard over their cars at night. The effort is definitely not the traditional idea of Italian chaos and temperament. It is a very smoothly operating team. Parts arrive air-freighted from Modena on the next jet in, anywhere in the world. They are backed by one of the world's largest motoring works, Fiat. James Hunt reckoned himself to be extremely fortunate that his car was not competitive for only three races in the season and that because of sheer bad luck. Ferrari try to reduce this.

It is extremely difficult to become a Ferrari race mechanic, almost as difficult as becoming a driver. An in-built hurdle is that you have to be Italian, because, as one put it to me simply, 'We are best mechanic in world.'

The only shared language which Coughi and Lauda have is English. This could lead to problems but does not. All orders come from Coughi to the other mechanics. He has been variously described as 'comic-opera Italian', 'lugubrious', 'cheerful', 'masterful', 'tactful' and 'volatile' by the sports hacks. He is a trim man in his early forties, a little shy about his position, but totally in command of his team of mechanics and unerringly precise about everything connected with the race car. His neatness extends to his person. Although I rarely saw him with his hands not inside the racing car adjusting this, changing that, I never saw a speck of oil on his clothes. My grandfather once told me that this was a sure sign of a master craftsman. He, I was told, could strip a steam locomotive in his Sunday best and only get his hands dirty.

Ermanno Coughi started his career, after World War Two, rebuilding motor scooters; caught the eye of an American, Carrol Shelby, and started to work on racing cars. Over the years, as his reputation as an impeccable mechanic grew, he tried to join Ferrari. He spoke to them, telephoned them and finally was invited to send in his curriculum vitae. This he did with alacrity . . . and Ferrari never bothered to reply. This oversight incidentally is now blamed on the famous Italian postal service, which at one point had such a backlog of undelivered mail that they simply burnt the lot. In 1972, through the then works team manager of Ferrari, Coughi was hired. He quickly worked his way up to chief mechanic for Formula One cars. He enjoys working with Lauda and has forged with him a friendship that is more than just mutual respect. He was at Nurburgring when Niki crashed. 'It was very very bad. It is difficult to explain. It is a cruel sport I tell you.'

They are both professionals and work very hard indeed. This was never more visible than at the Japanese Grand Prix. Because of Niki's crash and the new car, everyone had to work just that little bit harder to try and bring the new car up to the mark. It was not quite right at Mosport; a bit better, but still not there at Watkins Glen; then came the final deciding race of the season in Japan. The team was by now being pushed very hard. Hunt and the McLaren were the team to beat. The mechanics worked and worked.

Lauda was three points ahead of Hunt. The scoring system works as follows: nine points for win, six points for second, four points for third, three points for fourth, two points for fifth, one point for sixth. Any score by Lauda meant that Hunt had to do just that much better. At the track there were the normal accusations: Hunt had broken an agreement and arrived at the untried new circuit early, there was no such agreement and so on. Then finally the day of the race. The conditions were truly appalling. It is most drivers' considered opinion that in future, conditions like this will result in a cancellation of the race. Hunt was heard to say in a small voice, 'I'm not going to race.' In the end, after some indecision the race started, in fog and driving rain. There was a lot of emotion and work invested in Niki's car by his mechanics. He came in after two laps and pronounced the race suicidal and stopped. The tension amongst his mechanics was huge. They did not talk but you could feel the questions. 'What about *our* car, *our* work, *our* hopes?'

Lauda got out of the car alone. It was as though he had betrayed them. Then Coughi came around, looked at him and embraced him with great warmth and a sad smile. It was a simple honest gesture and in an instant all the tensions vanished and Niki was right. *He* was the driver and only *he* could judge how dangerous it was. Coughi had shown his mechanics that he still trusted and believed in Niki. As a matter of fact it was nothing short of miraculous that a large number of drivers were not killed in that final race of the year. Every driver after the race agreed.

What is it like being Lauda's mechanic?

'He is very demanding, but very precise. He can tell you exactly what needs to be done. Then we do it.' He paused. 'You could say he is a perfectionist. Yes.' Just a slight flick of the eyes heavenwards in supplication.

Despite the intense rivalry between teams, Coughi still has a refreshingly down-to-earth perspective on their role, which would horrify the ascetic Dr Forghieri ('. . . we are *not* part of the theatre').

'I tell you we are a travelling circus. We cannot be bad friends. Last night all the mechanics have a party and we all enjoy ourselves which is how it must be.'

None of the F1 racers does any mechanical work himself, although most of them could, if needs be. The reason for their mechanical knowledge is simple. When they started racing most of them had to be their own mechanics.

Scheckter: 'Well, I started building racing cars in my dad's garage. You get to know about engines.'

James Hunt: 'I started racing by rebuilding a Mini. I did all the jobs myself, got the bits and pieces from the knacker's yard. It was cheaper that way. You soon learn to be good with your hands, there's no other way.'

Lauda started on a Mini as well. 'I built a Mini. I know enough about mechanics. It is necessary if you are to become a top class driver.'

At one race I spoke to a mechanic/driver who is probably fairly typical of the end of the spectrum that these F1 drivers have left behind. The F1 work area was warm, dry and well-lit. Mechanics bumped and banged their racers into shape. It was cold and raining heavily outside, a fact of which almost everyone was oblivious.

Some way away was a large marquee. This was badly lit, wet, very cold, muddy and all it had was an over-abundance of air, cold and blowing in continually. In this area were the F1 hopefuls. They were all working on their Formula Bosch cars. They lay on their backs in the mud under the cars and froze and cursed. There was some speculation as to whether the tent would stand up to the cold gale. I remarked to one that no F1 drivers worked on their cars.

'I'll tell you something, buddy,' he retorted, 'if I had their bread I'd sure as hell hire me a mechanic and I'd be in some motel screwing a broad, not busting my arse out here.' He slumped back into the mud and shook his head.

An hour later James Hunt, warmly ensconsed in his motel, told me, 'Well, I don't get much time for women when I'm racing.' Between the idea and the reality . . . falls the shadow.

V

Racing

There is no safe way of suddenly stopping a car at 150 miles an hour. This is Forghieri's Law, Lauda proved it. Dr Mauro Forghieri.

Most races are run on circuits. Ideally this is a purpose-built track allowing the drivers to compete fast enough for spectator enjoyment without killing themselves. This might seem a simple thing. It is not. As cars change and become faster so the circuits which were built to cope with certain speeds become unsafe. The simplest solution is of course to build a circular track with walls and heavy chain link fences around it, mainly to protect the spectators and let the drivers go round as best they can. This is what happens at Indianapolis – but that, as most afficionados will admit, is not a test of driver's skill, but of driver's courage. He with the fastest car and the heaviest boot generally wins. F1 Grand Prix drivers have been known to race at Indy and win, but they don't make a habit of it.

The Armco fence has helped circuit safety a lot. This is a steel sheet supported by heavy posts set in concrete. The Armco fence was installed mainly because of the accident in Le Mans when eighty spectators were killed and on the insistence of the drivers in general, Jackie Stewart in particular. The race organisers were of course loath at first to erect these safety barriers but faced with ultimatums of no races from the drivers the steel fence was introduced. Ideally the fence should absorb some of the energy of impact on collision and not let the car off the track. A driver will now survive a head-on with the fence at 90 m.p.h. *provided* the fence meets with regulations about strength, supporting poles, bolts, washers, etc. Even ten years after the introduction of the fence there are still numerous tracks on the Grand Prix fixture list which are not up to scratch: Montjuich in Spain, Watkins in the U.S.A. The reasons are many and various. At the former track the condition of the circuit in 1975 was atrocious, with parts of the Armco fence protruding lethally into the track. Sections were bolted loosely and some not bolted on at all. There were heated exchanges between drivers (Grand Prix Drivers' Association, G.P.D.A., concerned mainly with track safety), the F1 owners (Formula One Constructors' Association, F.I.C.A.), · the Commission Sportive Internationale (C.S.I.) and the organisers. Some people go to an International Grand Prix and discover chaos, political intrigue, bad manners and downright cheating and are horrified. The more seasoned campaigners know that things are merely running normally. In this particular race (in Spain) the C.S.I. and the race organisers behaved abominably. Whether this is due to inefficiency, corruption, stupidity or all three is unknown.

The drivers refused to race; pressure was applied and some agreed to race. After an inadequate practice a number of bad-tempered drivers started. Lauda crashed on the first lap. There were other crashes, many more than usual and then one car killed a marshal and a photographer. It took the ambulance ten minutes to appear. An ambulance can be got almost anywhere in London quicker than that. Niki Lauda appealed personally to the organisers to stop the mayhem, which they did, after a while. There is a case for banning races from tracks where the organisation is so incompetent as wilfully to endanger life. There is also a case for imposing bans on organisers who by their greed and inefficiency aid and abet this. As Lauda said, 'It is not fair, they make money out of our lives.'

It is, sadly, almost pointless to look to the C.S.I. for firm guidance. It seems to be run by knaves and fools. Judgements are made and then overturned. Just lately their latest idea is that F.I.C.A. should not negotiate with circuit organisers directly about races and money, but through another organisation, partly staffed by C.S.I. members and a motley gang of ruffians (including an ex-Nazi) who will take a generous fee for something F.I.C.A. did on its own before.

As of now numerous races are being arranged by the C.S.I. offshoot and cancelled by F.I.C.A. (and vice versa). Someone has come up with a jolly wheeze to make money where they could not before (C.S.I. is a non-profit-making organisation by law). Money is of course the cause of most of the trouble. Today's Grand Prix racing is big money. It is expensive to enter; current reckoning is £$\frac{1}{2}$ million if you are serious and the returns, if you are successful, are equally high. Niki Lauda is a millionaire, Hunt is about to become one and other ex-world champions are equally well off. Without the money there would be no problems, the Catch-22 is that there would also be no races.

Another sidelight on safety is that the Armco fences which the drivers have campaigned for so strenuously are anathema to the other fraternity which uses the circuits – the motorcycle racers. They have of late refused point blank to race at circuits with naked Armco fencing. The fence, designed to cushion a crashing racing car, is totally lethal when a motorcycle rider comes off and hits it. To the unprotected human body its impact is similar to that of a brick wall. The organisers have to put straw bales in front of the Armco when motorcycles take to the track. Since fourteen miles of straw bales were impractical at Nurburgring the organisers baulked and the motorcycle riders staged their first strike in history.

Another innovation, in addition to the Armco barrier, is a safety fence. This is a chain link fence held by poles, which gives way progressively, more or less like a huge steel spider's web. It has drawbacks in that the support poles have a nasty habit of cracking the heads of drivers as they go by; also under certain conditions the chain link fence has been known to ball up under the racing car, giving it enough height to clear the Armco barrier. This happened to the unfortunate Mark Donohue while he was practising. A pole hit him on the head, which eventually killed him, and his car, mounting the Armco barrier, injured two marshals, one fatally. It is, as Ermanno Coughi said, a cruel sport.

Not all organisers are remiss; some, to the best of their ability, try to make the tracks as safe as possible. But sadly the totally safe track is like a good bubonic plague – an impossibility. The latest measure to make tracks safer is to put a wide ditch filled with pumice around the track. This friable, porous material has the effect of gripping the car and slowing it down rapidly. Ordinary sand cannot be used because when it is wet it compacts and is, if anything, worse than a slippery track.

Along with the fixed hardware of safety at a track there should be a number of other measures, chief among these being the medical and safety services.

The medical teams are variously organised but always include a doctor, nurses and, latterly, emergency medical technicians. Close by will be a well-equipped emergency operating theatre, staffed by specialists with all the equipment needed for diagnosis and treatment of fractures, traumatic ruptures and burns. As mentioned, a neurosurgeon could possibly have saved Mark Donohue's life had the ruptured blood vessel in his head been diagnosed in time.

A race casualty will be quickly X-rayed to determine what is broken and then he will be 'stabilised'. This involves keeping the patient alive and well while more information is built up as to what is not functioning correctly, and then applying appropriate remedial action. With modern high speed accidents the line between life and death is fairly clear. The trauma is either massive and fatal or some bones broken which will heal in time. We have the technology to do remarkably little when vital organs are damaged. There are no bionic racers. It is fire that presents the biggest challenge. Clearly in any accident, especially fire, it is of prime importance to get the driver out of the car and under surveillance. The life support services at most tracks pride themselves on their response time, which is always measured in seconds. This is why the period mentioned in Spain (ten minutes) can be fatal and is scandalous. I witnessed one accident in a Grand Prix where it looked very much as though the driver was about to die in a sheet of flame. There was the dull thud as the car exploded into flame, a gasp from the crowd as the driver, clearly visible, almost in slow motion, tried in that frozen moment to heave himself from death to life. Then suddenly there was a louder whoosh and the flames disappeared magically. The other racers flashed by as the fire marshals played the extinguisher over driver and car. It all took about four seconds, and the driver lived.

Every micro-second counts in an emergency like this. The fire extinguishers used are usually high expansion, liquid-based, foam compounds. Dry chemicals are not popular because as Bill Peters, fire chief at Watkins Glen told me, 'It puts the fire out, but it puts the driver out as well.'

The fire engines come in various sizes and there will be more than one around a circuit. The main fire engines will carry a man with a flame-proof suit. He can walk into the middle of an inferno and survive for a limited time. The fire engine will be backed up by a car carrying various hydraulic jacks that can pull, push and cut their way through just about anything to get a trapped driver out. The strangest of these is a hydraulically driven machine which looks like a cross between a giant's scissors and a crocodile's jaw.

'We call it Jaws, Jaws of Life,' said the laconic operator,

whose attention in this case was evenly divided between the long white thighs of the woman sitting next to him and the race.

These hydraulic devices are extremely useful in a bad pile-up. According to Jackie Stewart, his worst accident was at Spa, in Belgium. His car went off the track and finally hit a tree. This ruptured the petrol tank surrounding him and imprisoned him. The fuel leaked into the cockpit and there he sat and waited for the flames. There was nothing he could do. Graham Hill saw the crash, pulled up and came to his assistance, knowing full well that now he too could go up in flames.

He tried to get Jackie out but could not. By now Jackie was passing in and out of consciousness from the fumes and the pain. If a fire starts with your lungs full of petrol fumes you do not burn, you explode. This is where the 'Jaws of Life' could have cut through the debris and released Stewart quickly and efficiently. As it was, Hill had to run off, borrow a spanner from a bystander and laboriously undo some nuts and bolts to get Stewart out. That there was no fire was a miracle.

In an effort to minimise damage from fire, racing drivers also wear special clothes. These are not fire-proof, but fire-resistant. First of all there is fire-resistant underwear, then fire-resistant race suits, a flame-proof mask, gloves three layers thick and finally a crash helmet with a flame-proof bib. Since his accident, Niki Lauda wears three flame-proof face masks. The whole outfit, designed for safety, is extremely hot. This bothers every driver, 'Well you're perspiring just sitting there before the race.' Except Niki, 'For me this is not a problem, I do not sweat.'

Part of track safety is organised by the G.P.D.A. Towards the end of the season, as always, relations between the drivers become strained. When asked by Lauda to attend a penultimate G.P.D.A. safety meeting Hunt demurred, 'To hell with safety, all I want to do is race.' Niki: 'We have been friends but he broke the rules. If you break the rules you are out. No argument. After Brands James shouts at me. This is not right. He should respect me as a driver. We have a job to do, bad feeling only makes it more difficult. You see James is on the safety committee, I asked him to come to a meeting and he refused, this makes driving more difficult for everyone.'

In the end, however, when James won the world championship Niki came along to the tribute at Brands Hatch and James reciprocated by opening a motor show for Niki. The cause of the friction was not the actual racing, but rules. Lack of, too many, interpretation of – depending on whom you listen to.

It started at the Spanish Grand Prix, run this time at Jarma. Hunt won and then the Ferrari team, headed by a new team manager, who no doubt wanted to make his mark as well, appealed. The McLaren was wider than the regulations stipulated. Hunt was disqualified. It seems an open and shut case until you know that the McLaren was three-eighths of an inch too wide and the regulation was precisely one day old.

After fierce protests Hunt was reinstated as the winner. Ferrari were dismayed.

'McLaren must learn to obey rules. We do, so must they.' Niki Lauda.

Then came Brands Hatch. The Ferrari team sent over a host of managers, including ex-manager Luca Montezemolo, 'To guard Ferrari's interests against the officials.' At the start Clay Reggazoni, trying to pass his team mate Niki, caused a monumental multiple pile-up; Niki escaped unscathed. Reggazoni stopped, as did a number of others and the race was halted. Immediately the Ferrari managers insisted that Clay be allowed to restart.

James Hunt: 'The Ferraris hit each other at the first corner, then there was a chain reaction shunt and my car was damaged in the ensuing confusion. The steering was damaged but I recovered and was pottering around when they stopped the race. While they cleared up the track, my mechanics repaired my car.'

The mechanics replaced the entire front end of the car in under half an hour. Then the stewards decided that Hunt was ineligible for the race. An announcement to this effect was made over the public address system and the good, quiet, well-behaved, phlegmatic, British public went bananas.

'I was really rather proud of them.' Peter Hunt, James's brother. Newspapers, paper bags, cups were thrown on the track. Then empty beer cans. Then *full* beer cans. Something was definitely amiss. The fans invaded the track. The stewards hastily convened a meeting and announced that J. Hunt could race. Smiles all round. Hunt went on to win the race from Lauda. 'I'm proud to be British today.' Spectator.

Protest from Ferrari to C.S.I. against Hunt's re-entry into the race. One official pointed out, 'You petitioned to allow Reggazoni to race and he was *definitely* out.'

'Ah, but that is part of my job,' Montezemolo with a faint Latin smile.

'We have been racing for thirty years and we never make a protest. But this season we do. They are breaking too many rules.' Mauro Forghieri.

Hunt's victory was declared invalid and Niki declared the new winner. It is as well that this decision was not made public on the day. There would have been very little left of Brands Hatch. James Hunt: 'The rules and the facts are simple; the rule says that cars that are *running* when the race is stopped are eligible for re-entry when the race starts. It says nothing more. I was running. That's it.'

The C.S.I. also ignored the fact that a number of racers who re-entered the race were stationary after the crash. More idiocy comes in because of translation of rules. Does the exact translation from French in the relevant rule mean 'running' or 'racing'? The scholars are still pondering.

'There's nothing much I can do about it so there's no point in getting annoyed. All I can do is beat my fists against the wall and end up with sore fists. It disillusions me, the whole thing was a rigged decision, just plain back to front. It was reversed because of political reasons and pressure from Fiat. Agnelli owns them and Ferrari and most of the Italian press.' James Hunt.

'After Brands Hatch we get thousands of letters from England supporting our position.' Mauro Forghieri. This I think speaks volumes for the English sense of fair play and the inventive Italian imagination.

After Niki's accident in Nurburgring his first race was Monza. For Niki this was important, to see whether he could ever race again. 'To see whether I am psychologically capable. It is no use if I say to myself yes I am fit, I want to race but somewhere the brake comes on in my brain.'

In this race, only six weeks after he was given up for dead, Niki raced and came fourth. Hunt, in this race, slid off the track, into the newly installed pumice safety trenches. He got out of his car to inspect the damage, saw there was none and tried to get back into his car. Two fat, officious Italian marshals would not allow him. Out of car, out of race. To Hunt this was the second indignity of the day. At the beginning of the race he had been relegated to the back row on the grid because of an alleged fuel infringement. The racer's fuel was tested for octane number then the rule book consulted. This reads:

By 'commercial fuel' the F.I.A. intends to designate a 'motor' fuel produced by an oil company and currently distributed at road refuelling stations throughout one same country. May therefore be used all commercial fuels of the country in which the event takes place, with no other additive except that of lubricant of current sale which cannot increase the octane number, or water.

May also be used any commercial fuel which in France, Germany, Great Britain and Italy is of the highest octane rating, according to the Research Method of obtaining octane ratings.

If the above-mentioned fuel could not be easily imported into the country where the event is taking place, it may be replaced by another one of similar quality and with the same octane number (Research Method) – with a tolerance of $+ 1$ – specially made by an oil company. Whenever, in France, Great Britain, Germany and Italy, a new commercial fuel is made available which has a higher octane rating than those sold so far the oil company producing this said fuel shall give notice to the F.I.A. by a registered letter and this new commercial fuel (or its equivalent as specified above) may be used for racing 30 days after the registered letter has been mailed.

As mentioned, they cabled the C.S.I. for clarification and were told in effect to reconsult the rule book. Rather than disqualify those breaking the 'rules' they were placed in an impossibly difficult position to win, in the back of the grid. What actually was at fault, as was subsequently discovered, was the stewards' testing equipment. It was touch and go at the race whether an irate Hunt was going to belt the marshals and spark off an international incident. (The track was decorated with signs 'Down with the English Mafia.') He did not and walked angrily back to the pits.

It was against this background that Hunt refused to sit on the G.P.D.A. committee. The rancour, such as it was, was bread and butter to a few perpetually crazed racing journalists. At a press conference an Italian with a face that looked very much as though it was stamped on rather than shaved every morning asked Hunt: 'Were you happy that Lauda crashed?' There was a pause among the saner journalists and the goon smirked.

'Well, that's about average for the sort of stupid questions I get, but I'll try to answer it. I am never happy when *anyone* crashes . . .'

It was just an ordinary F1 season.

The Opposition

You have a thirteen to one chance of coming out alive, which is pathetic. Jody Scheckter.

A friend of mine, Ken Ashton, recently made a documentary for the Royal Air Force to recruit pilots. The film, in its final form, was rejected by Whitehall, much to Ken's annoyance. 'Bloody left-wing fools.'

The problem was that he discovered that to be a good pilot you need to be a good athlete, cut some dash and be fairly suicidal. Not exactly the image the R.A.F. wanted, however true. It was, as he pointed out, useless to try and recruit people on the basis of good retirement and pensions when the chances were that they would not reach the necessary age. Almost exactly the same can be said about Formula One drivers. It's a risky business. The racers know it and yet they are willing, for a certain amount of money, to take a chance. It is calculating to a nicety the value of your life. For most of us this is impossible. I may write a bestseller which will settle me for life; I may, on the other hand, trundle along modestly as most writers do, there are many imponderables. Not so the racer. If he comes in and wins he is set for life, financially. The problem is winning and surviving.

The man (or woman) has not been born who can step straight into an F1 racer and win. There is usually an apprenticeship of about five years and then if one is good enough, five years at the top. Then, if still alive, retirement at age thirty. Fangio retired to a profitable distributorship of Mercedes in Argentina, aged forty-seven, but he was an exception. It is easy to see why almost all drivers are politically conservative and wedded to the capitalist ethic.

To get to the top in F1 racing is no easy matter. There are no set routes and you usually have to do it all on your own, which may be another factor in the racers' conservativism, they tend to be sturdily self-reliant. Of course, on the way up sharp elbows and a little bullshit can help. I have before me a number of handouts given to the press about drivers. John Watson drives for First National City Bank Travellers Cheques Team Penske and is described by the aforementioned F.N.C.B.T.C.T.P. as, among other things, a ' . . . determined . . . clean Irishman'. John in fact comes from Belfast and must be one of a new breed. Most Irishmen I know are variously dirty in thought, word and deed (and sometimes body). The handout then spends a disproportionate amount of time on the team organiser Mr Penske, his life-style, his money, his houses. If you've got it, flaunt it baby.

Another handout was a glossy about Brett Lunger. This was interesting because there were rumours going around that he *paid* to drive. There are a number of drivers who pay to drive. This is no sin, more a sign of insanity. It is probably the size of Lunger's purse which the rumour-mongers dislike. He is a du Pont and could if he so desired probably purchase all the cars that race in F1 without altering his life-style. As a racer he was not particularly impressive, but to compensate for this his handout waxes lyrical: he was an ex-Marine Captain in Vietnam (which to many people is equivalent to bragging about being a Nazi) and has ' . . . in addition to his skill behind the wheel an image and presence still uncommon in this or any other sport – that of an aware, articulate spokesman. Whether it be a shopping centre or a high school . . . Lunger carries the glamour and excitement of Grand Prix racing with him, along with a masculine charm that reaches all audience levels regardless of their age, sex or racing knowledge.'

I spoke to a man claiming to be Brett Lunger, in what is probably the shortest interview on record. Three yesses, two noes, end of conversation. This one was also short on masculine charm, intelligence etc. etc. Beware Mr Lunger, there is an inarticulate harassed little man following you around who is doing your image no good at all.

What then makes a good F1 driver? I wrote a book on motorcycle racers (*Last of the Great Road Races*, Transport Bookman) a little while back. On this one point riders all had different opinions. There are a great many ways of riding a motorcycle fast around a series of bends. On this same point the F1 racers were usually reticent, not because they had anything to conceal but because the car will mostly dictate driving style.

'I have to throw it into corners, that's the only way it goes round.' Jody Scheckter talking about his six-wheeled Elf-Tyrrell.

Hunt was adamant that he could teach me all I needed to know in about fifteen seconds. But gradually a picture began to emerge, lacking perhaps the most conspicuous trait. This is, of course, courage. You have to have the courage to go out, week after week driving on the limit, knowing that any mistake, or mechanical failure, could be the last thing you perceive.

Besides this the top drivers need a will to win, almost a cruel competitive edge; they must be in the words of one team manager, 'Hungry Drivers'.

Jody Scheckter is a driver who, if he carries on in his present form, has a good chance of becoming world champion. He was born in South Africa, is short and burly with curly hair and a quick smile. He has quick reflexes – 'At tennis I can get to the ball quickly. I can't always put it over, but I get there on time' – but rates himself an average athlete in all other departments. He was useless at school: 'I was expelled, now they want me back on speech days as an example to the kids. You see, it's only me and Gary

1   Niki's silent concentration prior to a race

2 James Hunt preparing to race

3 Stirling Moss, guru of the track, speaks to Jochen Maas

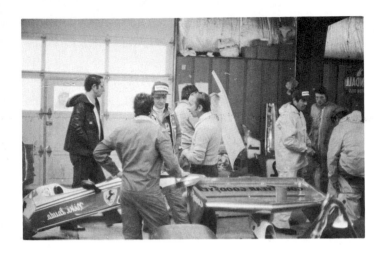

4 & 5   Race cars in preparation

6   This is at the centre of the mechanic's skill

7   Every mechanic has a task while Niki talks to the chief
    designer

8 & 9   Last-minute adjustments before a race

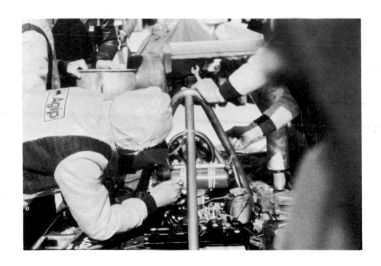

10 & 11   Wouldn't it be fun if this car banged that one?

12 In a crisis this spaceman is the driver's best friend

13 Niki at speed

14   While Niki races, Marlene waits anxiously . . .

Player who are the superstars in South Africa . . . internationally.'

As a hobby he started building racing cars in his father's garage, won some local races and then had a crack at international competitions when he came over to Britain. His début here was spectacular, although to hear him tell it in his flat South African accent, it was entirely normal.

'I crashed a lot in '73, that's why you heard of me. The biggest shunt was at Silverstone. It happened right in front of the pits in front of the press. Gave them something to write about for a change.' This was a spectacular multiple pile-up involving Scheckter and just about every other car on the track. The sports writers put it down to his 'aggressive inexperience'.

'That's a lot of bullshit,' said Jody. 'Motor racing is all about going quickly, but the edge between quickly and falling off is very close. You're very clever until you come off. Then you're stupid. What a rock ape, people say. If you go slow they don't comment at all.'

We spoke a little about his being Jewish. 'My mother worries . . . but then so do I' and then about what makes a really good driver. 'It's difficult, but what it boils down to is this, you've got to be good all round. Fast in practice because that gets you pole position, which is an advantage, and in practice you are not chasing anyone, only the clock. Then you have to be good in dry, good in the wet, good in "traffic", you know, getting through the field when you have to. Perhaps the most important thing is setting up the car before a race, every track is different and every car, and you have to get it right.' A fan appeared with his book, which he obligingly signed. He came back.

'Where were we?'

'Going fast.'

'Oh yes, one other thing is outsiders. People who are not very experienced, they're a bloody menace.'

Then the master of the multiple shunt proceeded to give me a lecture on being 'courteous' on a track and what 'good manners' in a race meant. Later I watched him race. He is very fast and very capable. At the end of the race he was laconic about his success.

'It was a good race, man.' He went off to relax, a process which takes him about three days.

He raced at Nurburgring in the race where Niki crashed, in fact he was one of the drivers who agreed to race when some were calling for a boycott. Was he perhaps too hungry?

'No, not really. We drivers signed a three-year contract to race there. I didn't feel we could break the contract. But racing is dangerous, we all know that. When we get paid as much as tennis players then it will be a bit fairer.'

James Hunt, another very fast driver, was also not a great academic at the public school where he was educated, Wellington. He was, however, a good athlete. 'But not out-standing – average reflexes, average eyesight.' The school gave him discipline. 'I didn't like it but it was good for me.' We do have an exceedingly curious educational system for those with the wherewithal. He raced the family car around country lanes until one shunt too many stopped that. Was he just fooling around? His head shot up and he stared at me aggrievedly. 'No, of course not, I was practising. I knew what I wanted to be.'

He built himself a racing Mini and then sold it. 'I sold it on the spur of the moment, all my best decisions have been taken on the spur of the moment. The money was just enough for a down-payment on a formula Ford which some enterprising gentleman was selling on the never-never. There was really no point in me even winning in a Mini because all I would have been then was a good Mini driver.'

From Formula Ford he went to Formula Three racers. Money, as with most aspirant racers, was a problem.

'This was just about the lowest point in my life. I had to go knocking on doors to get sponsorship and the doors were always slammed in my face. I was completely broke; I'd take any job just to get some money then it would all go on the car. I had no social life, I could not accept other people's hospitality because I could not reciprocate. My only relaxation was squash. The club had a beer kitty so I was able to get drunk once a week. That was it. The club members simply regarded me as a nutter.'

He signed on with March Engineering as an F3 driver but the partnership was not a success. He left after a row in Monaco and met Hesketh racing.

'It was quite funny really. I was looking for a sponsor and they were looking for a driver. "Bubbles" [Bubbles Horsley, Hesketh team manager] and I met in the middle of a field full of cowpats and for once I kept quiet and let him talk, which was great because it established our relationship from then on.'

Central Casting (Worldwide Inc.) could not have found a better matched driver for Baron Hesketh. James is blond, athletic, good-looking, good-humoured and most important of all socially, truly a gentleman. Watching him get rid of the various race groupies who were fairly explicit in their demands, was a revelation.

'I'd love to, but unfortunately I have made other arrangements for this evening. Really.' They left one by one, their smiles proclaiming to the world that James Hunt would have laid them if only he had had the time!

So Hesketh racing got truly under way.

'The rest of the racing fraternity were unimpressed. They had seen it all before. The private yachts, the helicopters, everything. We also had a homemade car which was a bit rude.'

By all accounts it was a happy period: 'Work hard and play hard, that was our motto.' But racing seriously in F1 proved more expensive than Hesketh had bargained for and on the very edge of success he stopped.

'I learnt a lot, mostly from Bubbles; he instilled a routine and a feel for racing in me which has stood me in good stead now. I don't really need anybody standing guard over me.'

67

How then does one become a fast driver?

'You get the quickest line through a corner and then drive the car on the maximum all the way. And don't lose it. Frankly, if you are intelligent there is nothing I can teach you. There is nothing you cannot work out for yourself. The difference is in execution. I have got a good sense of balance, which is perhaps important since racing is rather like skiing. You are always balancing the car in a corner. Feeling it. There is also a natural something in fast drivers which I can't define. It is easier to talk about bad drivers. They do not have enough aggression and they lack confidence. A bad driver on a new track will go around the track at five miles per hour, then six, and by the time everyone's gone off to bed he's lapping at a hundred and fifteen miles an hour where you should be doing one twenty. A good driver will be doing a hundred and fifteen on his second lap, because he will attack it and he won't fly off the road. He will attack it within limits. There isn't time for fancy practising.'

He denies that he was called 'Hunt the Shunt' because in his younger days he was more concerned with winning than safety. 'No, it's not true, mostly the name stuck because it rhymes. Besides, in F3 racing you do a lot of slip-streaming and if one goes they all go. Lots of multiple shunts.'

His worst accident was at Zandvoort where a car behind him lost control, hooked his wheel and flipped him over. 'I was skating down the track upside down, damaged my back a bit and made a couple of holes in my hands.' He had no problem in racing again. 'If you have any doubts you should not be racing.'

Was he ever scared?

'I don't get frightened when I am driving because if I am in a nasty situation I'm too busy sorting it out. It's cold calculation. If you're frightened you're not capable of looking after yourself, you're not in control.' He paused and then looked evenly at me. 'I'm frightened when I sit at home and think what can happen. *Then I get scared*. It's very worrying. I have to live with this thing. It's a big pain in the arse because I have a hell of a nice life. I'm in my prime now, having a hell of a good time, and there's this bloody great cloud hanging over my head. A real pain.'

Fear, paradoxically, plays a part in a good driver's make-up. There is a world of difference between being courageous and being fearless. The biggest difference is that drivers in the latter category are almost invariably dead. The Marquis de Portago was a good example of this. He had everything, Latin charm and good looks, a title, money, women. Everything except fear. In the end, because he knew no fear and hence could not recognise and react to a dangerous situation, he was killed. As someone said, he was 'an accident looking for a place to happen'.

'Being a G.P. driver makes you hypersensitive about danger, driving on an ordinary road, where I am very careful and all sorts of situations, like walking down a grassy bank when it's wet. I'm more careful about slipping and hurting myself than most people. There's more at stake for me I suppose. You could say I've become highly chicken about everything.' James Hunt.

Except when he gets behind the wheel of his racer. He has a set routine before a race, starting on the Wednesday before. 'It's a mental build up and is all to do with concentrating and getting myself in the right frame of mind and mood for the race. It culminates on race day when I am very nervous indeed.'

This nervous tension is one thing all race drivers share on race day. You can almost see the nervous energy bubbling off them as they move around constantly. Never in one place for more than a few seconds, then moving on once again.

James Hunt spoke about his friends. Like most superstars, his friends now are the friends he made when he was amiably regarded as a racing nutter. Then there is also the team that he races with.

'I get on extremely well with them, which is good because there are some drivers that don't. Like when I won at

Mosport we got into the motor home and drove to the motel and then we just sat gassing in the motor home, in the car park, all night. Nobody said we should stay in the motor home, it just didn't occur to any of us to get out, we were having such a good time.'

After the race there are other problems, especially if the racer wins. By the end of a race, the drivers will have been concentrating absolutely for just under two hours. Literally every second they will have been at full stretch, physically and mentally, with no let-up whatsoever. Then if they win they have to contend with the fans. As one driver explained: 'You've been concentrating very very hard; you have probably seen one or two of your friends in shunts, avoided one yourself either by luck or because you were watching all the time and took the necessary avoiding action. Well, at the end your adrenalin is really going and you're sweating like a pig and then the fans start grabbing at you. Physically pulling you and all wanting to talk to you at the same time. I don't know what the hell they want to talk about, they've just seen the bloody race, probably know more about it than me.' It takes most drivers three days to recover physically and mentally from a race.

James Hunt: 'It's very difficult, the only time I'm on my own is when I get into my room and lock the door. There's a temptation, when the seventy-fourth person grabs you and gives you an earful of bullshit, there's a temptation to tell him "Fuck off, will you, leave me alone", but that person's probably travelled three hundred miles and especially wanted to talk to you. You need their support and it's nice to have and it's not their fault they've caught you at a bad moment, they didn't mean any harm, you have to remember that. But sometimes it's very wearying, very tiring, quite heavy.'

This conversation took place in a restaurant which overlooked James Hunt's room. I was about to ask him another question when he interrupted me.

'Someone is trying to break into my room.'

We both looked down at his room. A good-looking, long-legged blonde was trying to climb through the window.

'Ah well,' he said philosophically.

The racer's life is just one damned thing on top of another.

VII

World Champion

All things oh priests are on fire...
The eye is on fire;
Forms are on fire;
Consciousness is on fire.
The Fire Sermon, Buddha.

He is a small man who does not know precisely how much he weighs, an Austrian, twenty-seven years old and a millionaire. He has cars, an aeroplane, a wife, and a house set apart, ringed by mountains. Such is the curious life of an F1 world champion that he has little time to savour the costly artefacts that his skill and courage have brought him. If he is not racing he is testing the new Ferrari at Fiorano in Italy or else travelling to a race circuit somewhere in the world preparing his car and himself for a race.

Niki Lauda comes from a prosperous middle-class family. His father, a retired business man, made a great deal of money as a paper manufacturer and by all accounts Niki had an extremely sheltered upbringing. People from his stratum of wealthy middle-class society almost invariably end up as prosperous professionals. Accountants, publishers, architects, certainly not professional racers. The very idea is horrifying. He has a more orthodox brother who is a medical doctor. His father is 'like an Irishman, round, jolly and red-haired. Niki gets his will power and determination from his grandmother, she was the strong one.' Marlene Lauda.

'The women in my life have softened my character, made me less obstinate.' Niki.

Relentless determination has also played a large part in Lauda's life. He was, like all other drivers, an indifferent scholar at school. Average athletically and average academically. Most drivers show this trait. There is something in their personalities that tires easily of book learning, is bored by lessons and is totally uncompetitive in scholastic ability. Niki completed his schooling up to the point where he had to take the university entrance exam. Then he decided to become a racing driver. Talking to him about this period in his life is difficult. Reading my notes I see that he answered my questions with monosyllabic yesses and noes, without volunteering any further information. If there are born losers, there are also born winners and they do not like talking about the time when they were not winning. Niki is also disconcertingly honest. There is no bullshit about him. He gives interviews but does not enjoy them. He realises that they are a necessary part of his life but cuts them off instantly when they begin to impinge on his time as a driver.

'As soon as I feel that as a racing driver I am losing out then I stop. Immediately. Because I am a race driver, not an interview giver or a television personality or an autograph signer. So when this happens I say stop. Then I go to bed, it is more important to be fit for my job, racing, than to appear on television or to be written about. I am the one who decides.'

His insistence on sleep is interesting; he does indeed sleep an average of ten hours a day, more after a race, and because of commitments has very little time left over for physical exercises, which *all* drivers claim they do, constantly. But then his driving style does not depend on brute force. More brain than brawn.

Another reporter, Heinz Pruller, commented to me after one long interview: 'I don't know whether it came over to you when he spoke to you, but he is precise and perfectly

logical in all his answers to questions.' The reason for
Heinz's doubts were because Niki's home tongue is German.
His English, however, is perfect. He never stumbled or
searched for a word and his answers were models of clarity
and precision. He is, unlike many sports people in the public
eye, understandably reluctant to turn all of his life over to
the public domain.

'I do my job racing and then I want my private life.'

Hunt, for instance, knows exactly what the media are
after and enters joyfully into the game. Fortunately he is
intellectually streets ahead of most of the people who would
advise or report on his persona. Hence, what he shares is
what he wants. He is also at some pains to conceal just how
intelligent he is.

Niki, on the other hand, is concerned with the process
of racing and is easily bored by the constant and mainly
mindless questions. Sample:

'Mr Lauda, could I ask you about your wife?'

'Yes.'

'Mr Lauda, is it true that when she first met you she
thought you were a champion tennis player?'

'No.'

'But I know when she first met you she thought you were
a tennis champion.'

'No.'

'Tennis player then.'

'No.'

'But I read this article which clearly stated that when
your wife first met you she thought you were a tennis champion and came up to you and said . . .'

'It is not true.'

'But this big article was printed . . .'

'That does not make it true.'

He looked directly at the reporter and waited for the next
question.

'Perhaps she *thought* you were a champion tennis player?'

'That you will have to ask her.'

So myths are made.

Marlene: 'He told me he was a racing driver and I did not know what it was all about. You see I saw him at a party and I thought he was nice so we spoke . . . but I had never watched a race before, so the first time I watched him race I was very excited and kept jumping up and down and asking everyone, "What's happening? Why are they doing this? Why are they doing that?" ' She smiled at a distant memory and then the smile faded.

'It was only later that I realised how dangerous it was.'

During a race Marlene is always at the pits, smoking constantly, trying very hard since Nurburgring to conceal her nervousness. Niki's former girlfriend, Mariella, busied herself as his official timer (besides the *official* official timer from Heuer).

Niki had, when he met Marlene, a girlfriend of some seven years' standing.

'I had a girlfriend before I met Marlene. And I loved Marlene more than her, so everything was simple then.'

There is a lack of guilt here which is either lamentable or praiseworthy. Tell me Sophie Portnoy what do you think?

He started racing, aged nineteen, in 1968 in a hill climbing Mini then went rapidly to Formula Vee (1968), then Formula Three (1970), Formula Two (1971) then in 1972 raced for March Engineering in Formula Two and Formula One. In 1973 he raced in F1 for B.R.M., in 1974 for Ferrari and he was world champion F1 driver in 1975. It sounds very easy but is not. The progress up the ladder to world championship status is never easy. There are untold thousands of amateurs who are convinced they could take the racer's place at any given moment. There are also thirty or so F1 drivers who would like to take your place and there are five or so élite drivers who undoubtedly *will* take your place at the slightest let-up or mistake.

Besides all the attendant dangers, fears and hassles of F1 racing Niki still counts himself lucky.

'I have always been interested in cars and so my job really is all that I want.'

But it is not enough to have latent talent; you need a machine. A fast reliable machine. Max Mosley of March Engineering was the first representative of the big-time teams to meet up with Niki, although at that time they were anything other than big.

'Niki walked in with £8,000 and said he wanted to race in Formula Two. This is not exceptional; if you are an unknown you pay to race, it's as simple as that. If you are known, you get paid and sponsors fall over themselves to get at you. However, Niki came to us and paid so we gave him a car. He was highly intelligent and very competent with a strong belief in his own competence.'

He also changed his physique immediately to race quickly.

'When I began racing my arms were too weak so I exercised them for strength.'

Then there came the hard grind of learning a race machine's infinitely subtle capabilities and learning the circuits.

'Ronnie Petersen helped me a lot when we were in March in this. Racing schools can also help a little, but then there is a point where you must help yourself. There is no one left to teach you.'

And then inevitably there were the accidents, especially in F3.

'Because you are all young and a bit crazy, but you must learn from accidents.' He had a bad accident in F3 the day Jochen Rindt was killed. The news of the death of the man who became world champion posthumously depressed him a great deal and he left F3 for F2 with March.

As his racing experience increased so also did one facet of his talent, an ability amounting to genius for analysing the race car's performance and behaviour. Niki can communicate precisely with the designers, mechanics and technicians the details of the car's performance. Communication is critical. In tuning to win races, very few drivers have this ability. Stirling Moss, whose ability to communicate is legendary, nonetheless won his races most often because he was a brilliant driver under all conditions of track and car. Jack Brabham and Bruce McLaren were designer drivers of outstanding competence. (Tragically McLaren was killed testing a car on which James Hunt's M23 is based, when the aerofoil broke away.) Jackie Stewart attained a very high level of communication with his mechanics, but of the present-day drivers Niki Lauda is in a class of his own. I heard one driver instruct his mechanics and designer.

'Well, I dunno, it's just not feeling right.'

On this sort of information the combinations for getting the car right are endless and the chances of success virtually nil.

Niki Lauda: 'I have a feeling about my car when I am testing it to get it right before a race. Some drivers do not. But with me I can feel. So we try this and that, rear wings a bit of adjusting. A small change here, a small change there. It helps perhaps a thousandth of a second and when it helps I go faster . . . and then I win.'

To understand how this is done it is necessary to understand not only the mechanical intricacies of the car, which paradoxically are probably the easiest to cope with, but also the subtleties of suspension and hence roadholding. With a certain prescribed tyre, this involves adjustment in braking capacities between front and rear brakes, adjustment of the front and rear aerofoil (bearing in mind the race circuit and the influence of the aerofoils on each other). Then the suspension dampers must be altered, the anti-roll bars stiffened or slackened, camber and toe-in changed. Each one affects the other and getting the precise correct mixture for any track is very demanding. Niki also knows with precision when the car is not on the limit.

On one track Niki was unhappy with the car's handling. They tried everything but still it was not right. Things in the Ferrari camp started to feel distinctly warm.

'The left handers are good but not the right handers.'

'But both sides are *exactly* the same adjusted,' said Ermanno Coughi, his voice just rising, his grammar going to pieces.

'No,' said Niki.

On Niki's insistence they stripped the car, a little reluctantly. They found that one of the front axles was slightly out of true from when Niki had clipped a kerb. New axle and smiles all round. You need confidence and knowledge to insist that you are correct.

I saw Lauda pull into the pits and then wait for Forghieri.

'I cannot go *into* the corner as fast as I want to, the car is losing it in the middle.'

'Suspension?'

'Slacken a little.'

'We cannot give you too much, how about altering the angle . . .'

'The rear suspension is just a little too hard.'

Then he sat there as the mechanics worked furiously around him, silent, in perfect repose, staring straight ahead, fingertips together as though in prayer to the mechanical god. His eyes were just visible through the holes in the flameproof mask, there was something fairly chilling about them.

This ability to know with precision what needs to be changed in a car, so necessary in a champion driver, can be construed as sheer bloody mindedness in a novice driver.

Max Mosley: 'Niki always had very strong ideas about the cars, *we* did not always share his ideas. We also did not think at that point that he had the natural talent to become a great driver. He would be competent.'

Niki's unpopularity at this time in the March racing team stemmed from his abrupt dismissal of the capabilities of their 'Revolutionary new racing car, the R721X, that was going to clean up everything'. As related, the novice Lauda was scathing about its roadholding, the very characteristic on which it was supposed to clean up all competition, while his team mate, the then more experienced Ronnie Petersen, approved of the car. With hindsight it is easy to be contemptuous of March, yet what team in the world will take the advice of the novice over the experienced driver, when the pressure is on at the beginning of the race season?

In 1972 Niki wanted to race both F1 and F2 for March. 'We needed more money from him to do this. He still had no sponsorship and Formula One is very expensive. In the end we settled for 2.5 million schillings (about £50,000). Niki borrowed this amount from a bank to give to us.'

Now if you know banks like I know banks, this is about as likely as the Great Train Robbers being elected Governors of the Bank of England. But more than that, Niki borrowed the money and promised to repay the sum plus interest *in five years*. This is real confidence in one's ability. How many people would borrow that amount of money, not as a confidence trick, but as a straight business transaction, putting one's talent and ability up as collateral. If you fail you fail totally. You are not just bankrupt, you are a washout. So Niki turned up at March Engineering with the requisite money.

Max Mosley: 'A week before the deal was to go through the bank backed out but Niki nevertheless signed the agreement and produced a guarantee from his father that the money involved was covered.' Max screwed up his eyes and looked impishly at me, 'It would be interesting to ask him today whether that really was a guarantee or a bit of paper.'

Niki, impassively: 'The guarantee was genuine.'

Max: 'In three weeks he managed to talk another bank into lending him all the money for the '72 season. Now he did two extremely brave things. He borrowed money from a bank which he couldn't possibly pay back and he gave the entire sum to a new English company which was on a very shaky financial footing. In that year Niki became the British F2 champion. He did not win the European F2 championship because his racer had inferior engines. Hailwood won that. In F1 he was a back-of-the-field runner.'

At season's end the usual shuffle of drivers took place and Lauda signed on with B.R.M., British Racing Motors – or as someone put it more accurately, British Racing Misery.

'Niki at that point felt a bit let down over us, I think. We would have liked to keep him but we could not get any sponsorship for Niki Lauda.' Max Mosley.

What does Max, with hindsight, now think of Niki?

'He is very much the sort of person to succeed in modern style F1 racing. He is capable and intelligent. He has a great deal of rapport with designers and mechanics. When he says he will do something he does it, he's not flighty. This business is serious, more serious than the outsider sees.'

What then are the qualities, the skills, the abilities that go to make a world champion F1 driver?

Niki: 'I have a more sensitive arse than other people.'

Besides his sensitive bottom what other attributes are necessary to be a good racing driver?

'You must be as precise as possible without emotion. If you have emotions while you are racing, say anger, sooner or later you will land yourself in trouble. You must remember you are driving on the limit all the time. There is no place for emotion in the precision which is needed. There is, of course, also only one limit. You push yourself over that in a modern racing car and you are dead. You must know what that limit is and work within or on it. To go beyond the limit is foolish. You have to learn to drive, say, at a hundred and sixty miles an hour one centimetre away from the guard rail instead of ten centimetres away. This is one of the things that makes a good racer. The other things, as I have mentioned, the technical work you have to know about and do, to make the car go faster.'

When pressed Niki will describe in considerable technical detail every aspect of F1 racing. What to do in all situations, in a corner: 'You brake at the braking point which you know from practice, not too hard otherwise the wheels lock. Stop braking when you are into the corner then use the throttle to accelerate out of the corner.' Easy!

'If the car is understeering then I brake *in* the curve which helps correct the understeer (i.e. back wheels drift around) but it is dangerous because if you brake too hard there is no method of correction and you lose it.' Not so easy.

'If the car is oversteering, then I drift it on the way out of a corner and let the rear wheel hit the side of the kerbing *and keep my foot down*, this throws you back, but can be dangerous.' Not at all easy.

'If you lose it through oversteer on a corner then you can do two things. Lots of throttle and if your tyres are hot, the engine will pull you out of the corner. Or else use the brakes and slide out. There is no time for choosing between the two actions and the decision is usually instinct.'

No, thanks for the invitation but I think I will stick to my old car. It does not go fast enough to do any of these things.

This technical precision also comes out in Niki's attitude to the media. He will give the technical boffins from the various specialist journals exactly what they want. How his engine/suspension, etc., is behaving, why, how and what modifications are envisaged. This is his and their job and there is a mutual respect. They are on the other hand mistrustful of the more flamboyant drivers like James Hunt. He should only talk about his car and not be confiding to the *News of the World* when, where, and whom he is screwing. Niki is more likely to become the village dustman than talk about his sex life.

His total concern is racing. What changes does this bring in a driver's make-up when he is racing?

'In a racing car you are a different person. You concentrate one hundred per cent. Some drivers when they spin out act crazy. This is only because the mind is still on racing. They are in a different reality, the racing reality. This is why they shout and scream. Sometimes it is ten seconds, sometimes it is hours to get back into the other world.'

Niki shot into the racing public's eye when he joined Ferrari. The almost perfect car and the near perfect driver

6   81

were combined. Niki was spotted by the then team manager when he was driving for B.R.M.

'They phoned me and I went over and had a look at what they had to offer.'

They had, as can be seen in the next chapter, a great deal to offer. Something for which all race drivers would trade their wives, girlfriends, their present and future fortunes, their mothers, fathers, anything . . . to race for Ferrari.

'When I was satisfied with what they had, I agreed to race for them.'

The cool confidence of Niki is amazing. Remember that at this point he was up to his neck in debt to a bank and was racing for a team that never stood the slightest chance of winning, no matter who was driving. But *he* was appraising Ferrari. He signed on the dotted line and fairly rapidly both his and Ferrari's fortunes changed. In 1975 he became world champion and Ferrari took the manufacturer's title after a long hiatus.

Inevitably when speaking to Niki one is drawn to his accident at Nurburgring, and accidents in general.

'I never have a reputation for crashing. I learn the limit quickly. In this business you have to push yourself hard all the way, all the time. There is no let-up. I can't go to a track and say I don't feel up to it today. You will be last on the grid and you have lost the race . . .

'I know motor racing is dangerous and so if I have an accident I am not surprised, because you drive a car on the limit all the time and if there is a minute mistake you fly off the road. At 180 m.p.h. in a Ferrari you are in a thousand pieces, you have to know this otherwise you are a fool.'

Before his accident Niki had had some bad moments at Nurburgring. It is an extremely difficult circuit to race, a fact which fascinated the technician in Niki, but very soon this fascination was replaced by a deep concern about safety at the track.

'At Nurburgring there are fifteen places where you can have a shunt and you are in big trouble. Most circuits have a maximum of two dangerous places. You know where they are and you take precautions. But Nurburgring has too many for this. They are not all simple things. It can be an unevenness in the track which gets you airborne and you have no control, or a corner where if you lose it there is no provision for a run off, then you are in trouble. You see, the race organisers get, say, between one hundred and three hundred thousand paying spectators. This is a lot of money. In return as a driver there are certain minimum safety standards which are laid down. Then you look at a track like Nurburgring and you know the safety standards are lower than that permitted by the rules. It is not fair to make money out of our lives. This is why there was a drivers' meeting before the race at Nurburgring, to decide whether we should race there. We had signed contracts, so we raced. But there will be no more races there again. This I know.'

Nurburgring is a circuit that arouses much the same emotions in car racers as the Isle of Man does amongst motorcycle riders: they either love it or loathe it. Both circuits are long, tortuous, arduous; both have claimed many lives in their history and both are undeniably bitches to race on. Modern racing technology is not suited to racing on a road which twists, turns, goes up, down, about and gets the cars airborne.

James Hunt: 'Nurburgring *is* dangerous. People criticise the drivers and say "Oh they're chicken" and "Not like they used to be" because they won't go to Nurburgring. But we'd love to go to Nurburgring when they make it safe. They say we won't race there because it's difficult and that's simply not true. It is because it *is* difficult that we want to go. At present it is unsafe and highly impractical. Now you can't race at a track like that simply because of sentiment. What about the other race promoters, whom we insist spend considerable sums of money to make the tracks safe? If they come to Nurburgring and see it they'll say why should we do it if they don't? Then nobody will make anything safe.'

But on that fateful day in August, despite his misgivings,

Niki raced. He raced and crashed, but this was no ordinary crash. First something happened, something which despite analysis and film nobody – not Niki, not the Ferrari team – even after a check up of what was left of the car can pin down.

Dr Forghieri: 'Nobody knows why Niki crashed, we checked the car but it doesn't seem to be the car.'

Analysis on Niki afterwards was a little easier.

'You saw the scars on his one wrist and the scars on his head and face. Well, the pole that he hit (supporting the safety fence) ripped his helmet and fireproof face mask off. That's why his face is badly burnt. The pole also ripped the racing suit off one arm – hence the bad burns on that arm.' Eye witness.

But the accident itself.

Forghieri: 'It is our opinion that the accident is caused by the very dangerous condition of the track from the temperature and humidity point of view. Niki was some fifty seconds from the pits and not enough time to warm up the tyres. He lost twenty seconds in the pit while they held him up. He was waiting to get back in the race.'

Perhaps for the first time, a little too anxiously.

'Something then happened – perhaps water and he corrected. Then he went into a spin and he went backwards into a fence. Unfortunately the fence was mounted half an inch away from rocks.'

Then another driver, Brett Lunger, hit him. He was into the corner when suddenly it was 'Just like driving on marbles. There were pieces of Ferrari everywhere and I had no control at all.'

He hit Niki at about 100 m.p.h. Then Harald Ertl hit Niki as well and there were flames and death came very close. Two other racers, Merzario and Edwards, managed to avoid the crash, stopped racing and four drivers converged on Niki. His helmet was ripped off, with it his life support system. By now Niki was unreachable because of the flames. An extinguisher was handed to Lunger, he pointed it at the Ferrari – nothing happened. He threw it back at the marshal who reprimed it and gave it back to him. It worked this time and Ertl was by now also operating an extinguisher, the flames died down, but not completely out. There were no marshals in flameproof clothing at hand. At some considerable risk to his own life, Brett Lunger mounted the wrecked car and tried to pull Niki out. But the safety harness would not spring free. Then the flames exploded searingly again. Lunger jumped off the car and after an eternity more extinguishers were turned on to the car. Lunger stood above Niki while Merzario loosened the safety belts. They hauled Niki free and he walked several paces, then collapsed.

'We didn't know how bad he was burnt,' said Brett Lunger. It would seem that the gentlemen who wrote about Brett Lunger's articulate machismo image are fools. All they needed to say was that he is brave and saved Niki Lauda's life.

'When we got him out he asked, "Is my face badly burnt?" ' Brett Lunger.

Just about this time Niki's wife Marlene was getting out of an aeroplane. She had been married for six months, had not yet met Niki's parents and was hoping to catch the tail end of the race. Perhaps Niki would win. There was a message for her. Niki had been hurt. 'Perhaps it was better that way, there was nothing I could do then, absolutely nothing, but go to the hospital. If I was at the track, I don't know what I would have done. It would have been worse, I am sure.'

At the hospital she knew that Niki was in a very bad way indeed. Only a short while ago they had everything; now it seemed, most horribly, all over.

But Niki did not give up and she did not give up.

'She was very good, she stood by me and gave me strength.'

There were bad moments when the priest gave Niki the last rites and the moment when the first photographer barged in to take the picture of the man who should have been dead. His face, then horribly burnt and not yet skin grafted, was the object of this particular photographer's interest and greed. We pay a lot of money to see other people's suffering.

But almost impossibly Niki lived, not because of medical science but because of something rather rare.

'There are no miracles in life. I stayed alive because I was one hundred per cent fit before the accident. I was fit because I wanted to be fit. I stayed alive because I willed myself alive. I recovered so quickly because I wanted to recover so quickly and I worked day and night for the recovery. We human beings have many resources of the spirit which we do not use. I try to use them.'

Niki maintains that this accident, this trial by fire and resolution by will, did not change him.

'I was concerned with surviving. It was very close for me, you know. When I realised that I would live – survive, then I worked to be ready to race. After a while I knew physically that I could race but psychologically I did not know if I could. It is easy to say "Tomorrow I'll drive flat out" but when you get into the car if there is something psychologically not right you lift your foot off. *There is a brake on in your brain.* This, not the car, will stop you. You have to make sure the brake is off in your head. I went to Monza to test this. After a few laps I started aquaplaning, which is quite normal, but I came in and said "no, I can't do it". The brake was on in my brain. But then I concentrated and it became better.'

For anyone who has never aquaplaned it is a frightening sensation, much like hitting black ice. You lose control of your car. If you are very, very good you do not lose total control all the time. You can retrieve the steering. But it is that odd, eerie, disconnected feeling when the steering wheel, a live bucking thing in your hands, suddenly becomes dead, it is then that you have to start thinking and acting very quickly or else you too are dead. It is highly significant

86

that Forghieri mentioned 'humidity', water on the track, as a possible cause of the accident and that Niki should emerge from the accident not bothered about mechanical failure, or losing it on a corner, or the hundred and one things that can go wrong and cause an accident. It is significant that he is bothered by *water* on the track. This is the brake that is now on in his brain. This is the one obstacle which he must tackle and overcome. A bitter aftermath of his Nurburgring crash. In Japan, in the deluge, he stopped racing. Conditions were too wet. So were they for three other drivers, but the rest of the field raced on. I would be the first to agree that Niki's judgement in withdrawing was rational. Rational, but not necessarily the correct one to keep on winning. But then it is easy to be a critic. He who lives by the sword dies by the sword, and I am unlikely to kill myself by falling on my pen. We demand not only winners, but supermen. Niki in some respects has become mortal.

After the accident the big thing for Niki was to see whether he could race at all. Six weeks after the accident he was at Monza.

'Because my car was destroyed at Nurburgring we were at a disadvantage. Racing cars need constant attention to bring them into fine tune. The new car needed a lot of work. Polished, you could say, continually. Like a bright piece of metal that goes rusty if you do not polish it continually. We lost step with Nurburgring and we had to work twice as hard to get back again.'

At Monza when he finished racing there was blood inside his flameproof mask. The scars from the fire and operations had opened up. He made no comment on this.

How did Marlene, who is so full of life and joy, view Niki's going back to racing so soon at Monza?

'Sure I get worried, but I control it. Monza did not worry me particularly, Niki is good as a driver and he would not do anything foolish. I was more worried at one race before Nurburgring. At the Spanish Grand Prix. Niki had an accident at home, a tractor fell on him and crushed some of his vertebrae and cracked some ribs. I knew how much pain he had, then I was very worried.'

It was about this race that he said, 'I could feel my broken ribs grating together. There was pain especially when Hunt passed me and I hit my broken ribs on the side when I swerved. I knew then I could not win.'

Niki came second in that race. Any orthopaedic surgeon will confirm that the pain involved in merely sitting up with crushed vertebrae and ribs is unbearable for the run-of-the-mill patient. You are sedated and given pain killers, laid flat out on a special bed and you do not move. With luck you will be out of hospital in a month and walking, very painfully, in two. The whole condition takes about a year to 'stabilise', i.e. become pain-free.

Niki, with crushed vertebrae and broken ribs, sat up and *raced* within days.

'I am paid to race, so this I must do.'

Lest anyone think that an F1 car is a soft ride, it is not. You are strapped down in your tailor-made seat precisely because of the buffeting your body is subjected to. Drivers have been known to stop a race because the seat did not fit them exactly, causing undue discomfort. I sometimes wonder what it will take to stop Niki racing.

Would it not have been better to rest, to recuperate for longer after Nurburgring? It was a very short time after the near fatal accident that he raced. Perhaps it would have been better to wait for the next season, there would have been less pressure.

'Pressure from other people I do not care about. I put my own pressure on myself to do my job. I never let people put pressure on me because *I* have to take the decisions in motor racing, not other people. I took the decision to race at Monza for reasons that I have explained.'

At this point in the talk Niki's then team mate, Clay Regazzoni, walked up to us and invited Niki in sign language (Clay speaks only Italian) to come and join him in a game of golf. Niki demurred.

'I am here to race, not to play golf.'

Then he waited for the next question. He is indeed a very talented and dedicated driver. More than that, he has the intelligence and single-mindedness that are essential to become a world champion. It has been said that it is easier to walk on water than become world champion. It is also admitted that the former skill requires less concentration and dedication.

Before one race I watched a man wish a silent watchful Niki 'Good luck for the race'.

'I do not need luck,' he said. 'There is very little luck involved in winning a Formula One race.'

And then they were off with a roar. He won.

VIII

The Racer

Talent alone is not enough, to win you need a good machine. Niki Lauda.

For its drivers, Ferrari has the finest test facilities for race cars in the world. All motor manufacturers have test facilities of varying size and complexity. Test beds for the engines where they drive them to, and into, destruction. Circuits with humps, lumps, puddles and bends to check the cars' roadholding. Only Ferrari has a purpose built race track to test race cars. This 1.8 mile track, in Fiorano, is equipped with the normal medical and fire fighting equipment. Testing is by its very nature dangerous and an uncomfortable number of race drivers have been killed testing. In addition to these normal trackside facilities, Fiorano has everything that modern technology can provide to analyse why a race car is, or is not, going fast. Ten video cameras stationed around the track with playback and freeze frame facility. Digital timers, graphical analysis of acceleration, instantaneous velocity at any point, speed around corners, interval speed, overall speed. Everything to ensure that the car is as close to perfection as possible every time it races. This track has never been just an advertising showpiece (as many other circuits are for the big manufacturers), it is used extensively and mostly in great secrecy.

It is the perfectionist's dream and Niki's delight.

'The facilities at Fiorano are perfect for testing, better

than anywhere else in the world. I could never drive for any-one else now.' Niki, before relegation.

Here he drives, studies times, alters a detail, studies times again. Does it improve things? Yes, good, on to the next change. When you are looking for a thousandth of a second improvement, the gradual elimination of error is strictly a scientific process.

In contrast to this is another race machine, that of twice world champion, Emerson Fittipaldi. His car has suspension problems. Or rather (in the nature of the team), it has sus-pension crises. So every third race or so the car is redesigned and glowing reports are issued – *now* the Fittipaldi-Ford Copersucar will be a world beater. It limps home and takes a terrible pounding in the Brazilian media. (A special broadcasting unit follows the woebegone team around the world and in Brazil there is a huge campaign in the press, radio and TV to get Emerson a faster car. 'The shame of the Nation' as it is headlined. They take their racing very seriously in South America.)

The designer, Divilia, then announces another design and has himself photographed at the drawing board to prove it. One journalist remarked that this car was designed on the Shakespeare-monkey theory: if you gave a million monkeys a million typewriters and let them bash away, statistically one of them has to come up with the works of Shakespeare – given enough time. And there's the rub, time. Fiorano, with its swarm of technicians and mass of technology, cuts down the chance, cuts down the time expended in arriving at the correct solution.

Some drivers understandably are bored by practice, e.g., James Hunt: 'It's a bloody drag. I do it because I have to do it, but I'd rather not.'

There are no crowds, no victories and only one opponent, the clock.

'I could get bored but all the time I am thinking ahead to what to do next and how it will influence the car finally.' Niki.

Hunt, in common with all the other drivers (Ferrari excepted), tests his car at the most convenient circuit, which is hired for the day. At Ferrari the number one driver has prime call on the track with all its facilities. His team mate uses up what time is left. It was a bitter moment for Niki when he, the world champion, the supreme tester, had to defer to Reutemann who was (briefly), made chief driver. But with minimum testing, Niki managed to convince Enzo Ferrari that *he was* the man to pilot his machine to victory. This juggling of personnel, or internecine warfare, as some would call it, is nothing new in the Ferrari team. They actually succeeded in giving five-times world champion Fangio a nervous breakdown when he raced for them. The pressure on Niki to win now must be quite extraordinary, which may be what led him to say, 'One day I may suddenly decide that it is all crazy, then I quit.'

At the test track there are broadly three categories of testing. Firstly the new race machines are tested, secondly the effects of any modifications on the car are assessed and finally they test the training car, which is in effect a reserve car to be used if anything drastic happens to one of the race cars. During this latter time, they also run in new brake pads. This is vital since you cannot simply use a brake pad straight from the manufacturer. It is put on to the brake caliper and the driver warned, usually with some pre-arranged sign, that he has new pads on. He will then drive and brake hard, deliberately overheating the pads until they are at the right temperature, which is signalled by a heat sensitive paint. When the pads are hard, with the correct surface, they are right for a race. Correctly run-in pads should last a complete race with no brake fade. If you overheat the pads, they disintegrate under pressure. Under-heating leads to loss of surface friction and less braking efficiency. It is not generally appreciated that races are won and lost when a driver makes a minute mistake on one braking point, the point at which he brakes upon going into a corner or curve. It is also, by the nature of racing, the last possible moment at which he can brake. For this point to be exact, lap after lap, the brakes, discs and pads must all be perfect, all the time.

The big tests are of course on the new machines, the new model, usually an accumulation of years of work by a dedicated team of designers, engineers, metallurgists, draughtsmen and mechanics. As with all new models the small things that inevitably go wrong are first to be corrected. The air scoop that is cracked, the switch that is permanently off or a small mechanical mistake which will not reveal itself until the race car is pounding away at 11,000 r.p.m. and 150 m.p.h. That is when the oil return flow pipe shakes itself loose because it was not secured properly. After the minor mechanical things have been dealt with, there comes the major testing. The effects of the rear aerofoil's angle of attack on the cornering and the car's speed will be appraised.

Then there is the front aerofoil . . . and the influence on steering of the back aerofoil on the front aerofoil. During this period the mechanical performance of the engine will be appraised. Is it delivering the predicted power, is it reliable, are there any modifications which will improve its performance? As always the proceedings will be enlivened by the unexpected. In one particular instance, when after days of testing the aerofoil was not working at all and when the designer was wondering whether there really was life after death, the cause was discovered. An oil cooler had been shifted on the chassis. This changed the airflow characteristics over the rear of the car which in turn created a turbulent flow of air over the aerofoil (which needs a streamlined flow of air to work correctly) which finally no longer gave the desired downward thrust.

Lauda regards himself as an integral part of the design team at this point. He advises changes, all of them carefully thought out and detailed.

'The first 312 we tried something, I made a suggestion. In this way I helped with the development of the car a lot.'

'Niki is very good, very competent. One hundred per cent professional.' Dr Mauro Forghieri.

So the endless testing goes on – roll bars, suspension, engine, gearbox. With a great deal of persistent work, intelligence and some luck the new model starts working well. The times are better than ever before. 'When it is all going well, I do not need a clock. I can tell!' But occasionally it all comes to nothing. Forghieri had spent a great deal of effort on a modified rear suspension, based on the de Dion rear axle, a design nearly one hundred years old and still universally used. But this time he lost.

'It was good. But not better than the one we had, so we dropped it.' Niki.

After the testing of new models comes the testing of modifications to the existing model, for speed and/or efficiency.

Ferrari does not publicise how much it spends on its race programme but it is believed to be in the region of £1,500,000 a year. With new models constantly being developed, a continuous test schedule, replacement of worn-out chassis, engines and occasionally drivers, the money gets eaten up quickly and it all focuses on a man and a machine, waiting on a grid for the flag or a green light.

Niki takes pride in the fact that here he usually has pole position. This premier position in the grid goes to the man with the fastest practice laps. Like playing white in chess it gives you an edge over your opponent. As the Russian Grand Master Mikhail Botvinnik put it, 'When I have white, I win because white has the advantage . . . when I have black I win because I am Botvinnik.'

The word practice makes it sound easy, much less dangerous than the race. This is not so. The driver, car and team arrive at the track which Niki will have assessed professionally.

Niki does not favour one track over another. Except of course for Nurburgring which he now actively hates, simply because he regards it as totally unsafe.

94

'This is the one track where the cars take off because of bumps. It is possibly good for the spectators, but it is not good for the car, they are not built to fly and it is very unsafe for the driver.

'There is no question of liking or disliking a track. I try to race every race with the same attitude. I cannot arrive at a track and say I do not feel like racing here. If I am not happy with a track I overcome this in practice by analysing why and when I am not happy.'

On arrival, Niki sets out to inspect the track. Have there been any alterations since last year? A new chicane (usually designed to slow the drivers down and avert accidents, but sometimes, because of careless design, having just the opposite result) a wider run-off area. Is that lump on the curve still there? Are the catch fences adequate?

All the top drivers go over the track in minute detail. This is where the experienced driver has a huge advantage over the novice starting his F1 season.

Niki has an extremely good memory for every track he races on. Danger areas, inflexions of the track, the successions of curves, braking points, wet and dry, the ideal line, where you can pass, where you can be passed. His memory is precise, mathematical in its precision, and seems to unroll like the replay of some film in his mind. He can point out exactly where his car will be on a track and at what speed his engine will be turning over.

Racing was not always as exact as this. Years back when both cars and tracks were much rougher, there was much argument about the tracks and the ideal line around them. Every new winner would usually attribute his victory to discovering a new ideal line on one or more of the corners. The pundits would gravely discuss the implications of the new ideal lines. Nowadays with fast cars and fast circuits, things are different. 'All this stuff on the ideal line is bullshit, if you can't find the ideal line you should not be racing.'

The ideal line ' . . . is the natural line where the car wants to go around a corner.' Niki.

The ideal line is the quickest and the best line around a corner for a *particular* car. Because of oversteer, understeer, tyre heat and so on it will vary a *little* for every car. But not a great deal. Outside of the ideal line, life for the driver becomes difficult, not just because he is on the point where his car becomes unstable but also since most cars follow more or less the same line at speed, they will sweep a path on every pass. The débris, bits of machine, rubber and dirt are on the outside of this swept corridor. Because of this, tyre adhesion off the ideal line is drastically reduced. This is one of the reasons why passing a car at speed on a corner, off the ideal line, is so difficult.

So at the track the race team and driver set up, and then prepare for practice. The general order of practice is: tune car mechanically, tune suspension and then make an attack on the lap times in the last day of practice. The track, say Paul Ricard, will have a fine layer of dust on it, a natural wind-born accumulation. The cars, even if perfect, cannot reach top speeds because of adhesion problems posed by the dust. But gradually, as the cars race around, the dust is dispersed and attacks on the lap time are started. All being well, the most serious attempts on lap time will begin on the final practice.

In Monaco exactly the reverse is true. Because Monaco is a road in constant use, there is no dust. What also happens is that at the end of three days' practice in Monaco, the road is slippery with oil and rubber, so here the best lap times must be put in on the first session, imposing a considerable strain on cars, drivers and mechanics. Also if you do not get pole position at Monaco your chances of winning the race depend less on skill and more on mechanical failure of your rivals. This is because Monaco is such a tortuous course, with very little opportunity to pass anyone, anywhere.

But at a normal practice the driver will spend the first

day tuning the chassis to the track and seeing that the gearing is correct. Assuming normal weather (i.e. dry) this will continue into day two but now the pace is hotting up. The weather can, and often does, wash a practice session out. Even if it does not, times in the wet will be lower than times in the dry. So the pressure is on virtually from day one. As the car and chassis come progressively into tune, Niki prepares for his assault on the lap time. With only a little petrol in the tank, he will go out and do one or two laps to warm up the tyres. He knows with some precision at this point what his rivals' times are. Now he puts in his bid.

'I wait for the traffic to be right, this is important because a slow driver can ruin your lap times if he does not give way, then when it is all right, I go. Now I drive with utmost concentration and take most risks. Drift over kerb stones, which in a race I would never do. I am now giving my best. When things go well, I don't need a signal from the pits to tell me I was good. I just know. Then I stop unless another driver puts in a better time. Then you have to go out and try again. But sometimes it is not possible to push the car more.'

In practice slow or uncooperative drivers who do not give way are a particular nuisance and likely to be remembered with asperity by those fighting for pole position. James Hunt was particularly incensed at being blocked by one driver: 'I treated him as a normal sensible person and he fucked me up. Niki treats him as a half-wit and the man respects him for it!'

After the final practice times have been clocked, the grid pattern for the race will be determined. Now the tension starts to increase as every driver focuses on the two hours ahead on race day. There will be the usual apprehension over the weather, a car set up to race in the dry will not be anywhere near perfect in the wet.

Niki with typical thoroughness now goes and talks to the starter. This is an elementary necessity which most drivers ignore. Niki wants to know how the man will start the race. Flag folded up and then sharply down, or one movement, or whatever. This simple question is vastly important. Mario Andretti and Scheckter at one race in Sweden misinterpreted the starter's motions. He had just started to lift the flag and they were away. The starter was merely lifting the flag prior to dropping it. Andretti was penalised one minute, which put him out of winning. 'Hell man I saw that flag move and I was away. This is Formula One racing and you don't fuck around. When that flag moved I dropped the hammer.' Latterly many tracks have installed a green start light which eliminates any ambiguity.

After his talk with the starter, Niki returns to the pits and is strapped in with his six point harness into the cockpit. This harness is particularly important. It must be tight enough over the legs and shoulders to afford maximum protection in a bad shunt and yet not so tight as to impede movement while racing. Harness adjusted satisfactorily, the engine is started and the warm-up lap completed. This is important for both tyres and engine. Warm tyres for maximum adhesion and warm engine to get the oil circulating freely and for maximum power. The warm-up lap also heats up the gearbox oil which, when cold, makes changing gear extremely difficult. More so because the gears are not syncromeshed and rely on crisp precise changes with double declutching every time. After the warm-up lap the mechanics rush out to do any final adjustments, then the engines are stopped.

At this stage Niki prefers to be left alone, indeed insists on it. In the complicated chemistry which goes to make a top race driver he needs these final minutes to get his mind absolutely concentrated on the race ahead.

'There are no emotions now, which is as it should be. Emotions stand in the way of winning. My mind is now totally concentrating on the technical details of the race. A race is after all a situation of changing technical problems which must be solved. The more the various possibilities have been thought about, the quicker and better you will be able to deal with them when they occur.'

Then the engines are restarted and they roll to the grid. Niki immediately disengages gear and keeps the engine at constant revs, in neutral. At the ten second sign he puts the car in gear and the revs go up. The ten second sign means that the race will start *within* ten seconds. Now everyone's adrenalin is pumping furiously and in their flameproof clothes they will be sweating copiously with heat and tension, all except Niki who stays cool, literally.

This is a tense moment in more ways than one because the race cars have just so much clutch and no more. A second or so over the limit and the clutch starts to engage from the heat and the car can roll forward off the grid.

Some drivers blip their engines. Niki does not. He will be watching the flag or the light like an eagle.

'It is always most difficult in pole position because there you can make a mistake and everyone sees you. It is easier if you are in the pack, then you just do the same as everyone else.'

Then the flag drops and they are away.

Niki takes off at 8,000 r.p.m. which he reckons is optimum for the car. Because of the huge amounts of power in reserve, the throttle needs to be used judiciously otherwise forward speed will be lost as the tyres burn themselves upon wheelspin. Once the tyres do bite, Niki has an advantage over all his rivals – more power.

'There is no way I can out-drag the Ferrari once we start rolling.' James Hunt.

The race has begun and all being well Niki will be up among the leaders. If he is not the leader then he starts planning to overtake his rivals. The problem is that even if you are Niki Lauda, passing another top class driver is difficult. The first thing to do is to exert pressure even if no clear opportunity to pass exists then. 'I will study him and then will start to irritate him. Always in his mirrors, this side then that, then I will work out the corners on which it is possible to overtake him.'

Corners which are too slow and too fast are ruled out. Both cars will be travelling at the same speed on the slow corner and on the fast corners, approaching too near into the slipstream destabilises the steering of the following car considerably, as explained. So Niki waits and harasses his opponent. What he is aiming for is for the opponent to make one mistake. With someone hounding you all the time, this becomes only too easy. If the driver loses concentration for a micro-second he will miss his brake point. This miss will mean that his line on the corner is no longer ideal, the fastest, and that is where Niki will pounce and take him.

Conversely, if another driver is trying to overtake him, Niki studies him as he comes into view. On which corners is he faster, on which is he slower? 'Then on the corners where I am slower I drive on the maximum, flat out, and I slow down on my fast corners.'

In this way Niki has a speed reserve on his fast corners which he can use at any time and on the corner where he is going all out it is extremely unlikely that the other car will be able to get anywhere near him. On the straights Lauda will go from side to side, baulking the other driver. This wins no points in the popularity contests but is legal and wins world championship points – and of course money.

Race lap times will very rarely equal the best practice times. This is because of a number of factors. At the beginning of the race, all the cars are burdened with full petrol loads which slow them down. As the race progresses and the fuel loads lighten, speeds generally go up. But then other factors come into play. As various engines blow up they spill oil on the track pushing up times for the other competitors. As the laps unroll, more rubber becomes deposited on the track, making it slippery, and finally the engines, tuned to perfection at the start of the race, start losing power, in the case of the Ferrari, some 20 b.h.p. These are the factors that most spectators will be unaware of.

There have been some races where Niki started in front, stayed there and won. Ideal races one might think. Niki recalls a few of these races and paradoxically does not like them all that much.

'For two hours all you do is listen to your engine and watch the instruments. You must be careful not to get nervous and make a mistake. These races last forever.'

One such race was Zandvoort, boring in the extreme for Niki but with a fair amount of chaos in the pits. The then team manager Luca Montezemolo, the man who first brought Niki to the attention of Enzo Ferrari, jumped into the pit stop road and was promptly run over by Ronnie Petersen. Exit team manager, but the pits still continued to signal to Niki how far ahead he was and how many more laps there were to go. Both bits of information Niki regards as vital and becomes markedly upset on the very few occasions when things go wrong. This is because he has a well developed philosophy of driving to win: 'You must drive only fast enough to win, no more.'

He regards pit information as a vital link in this process. If for instance he is nine seconds ahead with nine laps to go he will then adjust his speed so that he loses a second a lap. He will win by an amount consistent with the smallest output of effort all round.

What has been described up to now is the work that goes into a normal practice and race. Things however can and do go wrong. After the final warm-up lap all tyre pressures are checked. Tyres have been known to lose pressure, in which case the race starts with one cold tyre and three hot ones. Under these conditions there is no way a good clean fast start can be made. Worse than this are changes in the weather. A suspension tuned for a dry circuit is almost the opposite to that needed for the same circuit, wet. This among other things is why Nurburgring is disliked. Parts of the course can be dry and suddenly, without warning, wet patches appear.

Generally, the suspension must be softened for a race in

the wet (as well as the major change of fitting wet weather tyres). For more adhesion in the wet more wing will be given to the rear aerofoil.

But worst of all is setting up a car for a dry circuit, starting to race and then having to cope with heavy rain. Then the car comes in to the pits, stops at a predetermined point and the engine is switched off. This is important since the F1 cars have no radiator fans, they cool only when in motion. More than one overtense driver has been known to blow up his stationary car in the pits, overheating it. The car is immediately jacked up and all four slick tyres changed for ribbed, wet tyres. There is no time now for changing aerofoils and suspension. Just over fifteen seconds elapse and then the chief mechanic signals the car off.

Driving becomes particularly difficult now, the car will be braking too fiercely and caution has to be used on the brake pedal. In addition to this, new braking points have to be worked out as the race progresses. Any mistake and, on the extra slippery surface, the car is certain to spin out. The other problem in the wet is the enormous rooster tail, kicked out by the cars ahead, reducing visibility to a nerve-shattering minimum. And finally there is the problem of aquaplaning when the puddles on the track become extensive. But that is part of the racing driver's lot. Then after all the hazards, all the exhausting concentration, manoeuvres, comes the chequered flag, the obligatory champagne (which, it can now be revealed, Niki *never* drinks: he pretends) and then the 'switches' go off. 'I relax, I go to sleep for a day. Sometimes this is not possible. When I first started racing I over exhausted myself, but now I am more careful. I plan carefully, sleep is important.'

Until his near fatal accident at Nurburgring it would have been easy to end this chapter, for Niki was winning virtually every race he entered. But then came the crash and questions were raised, not least by him. Could he go out under *all* conditions and virtually guarantee to win? For this you have to push yourself to almost superhuman limits of physical endurance, courage and driving skill.

Suddenly racing and winning became more than the precise unemotional events in the very talented Niki Lauda's life. The pressure, because he *was* world champion, because of Ferrari and mostly because of himself, is at a pitch that will now either make or break the man.

Watkins Glen

It's not only the races, it's the people. John S. Yarrington, less and less distinctly as the night wore on.

To get the full flavour of Formula One racing it is imperative to go and watch a race. To savour the moment of perfection, better still go to a race far away and arrive some days ahead of time to see and appreciate the men and machines.

I travelled to Watkins Glen in America to see the penultimate race of the year. You fly from Heathrow with about two hundred other race fanatics and arrive at sunset at Kennedy Airport, New York. If you are even more obsessed than normal, you hire a car and head for Watkins Glen. Then because you have a map which was probably drawn by Dali you drive around for a while until it dawns on you that you are not only lost, you do not even know in which direction you are travelling.

At this juncture you are probably a little nervous. New York is made for motor cars, motor cars which are travelling fast and purposefully. Motor cars which show they are veterans by the number of dents they have collected. Your nervousness is exacerbated by the hooting, shouting and cursing that follows you around. But you say to yourself that you must stay calm and do not get upset when you find you are driving on the wrong side of the road or looking right when you edge across an intersection and a car travelling fast nearly hits you from the left! Consult your map, get on to a freeway and drive. In the end it is all too ridiculous and you have to stop and ask someone the way, get a proper map, soothe your nerves, end the farce. So you get off the freeway again and stop in a pool of light. People stop anywhere all over London and ask the way, what more natural, then, to repeat the process in New York?

As I got out of the car and locked it, it was the smell and the rubbish heaps that I noticed first. Then the things standing silently at every crumbling doorway turned out to be people. Smoking, watching sullenly. And suddenly for the first time in many years I was very scared. Two youngsters materialised out of the shadows and made for me. To run under these conditions would have been fatal. So I watched and waited. If they moved out of my field of vision I decided I would have to take on one of them. Quickly. They stopped just where I could see both of them.

'Hey, you wanna buy a reefer, man?'

I blinked. 'No, I want to get to Watkins Glen.'

'Reefer, man,' said the other.

'Watkins Glen,' the first youngster pronounced it as though it was a philosophical concept. 'Hey man, that somewhere near Flushing?'

'I don't know,' I said.

'Sure you doan wan a reefer man?'

'Anythin' else . . . smack?'

'No, thanks though.'

They shrugged and walked away. All the time the men in the dark doorways did not move. Had there been violence they would not have moved either. I unlocked my shiny new car and drove away. Any way, just out of the helpless, mindless despair that I could see and feel in Harlem, New York. I remembered an I.B.M. computer programmer telling me, 'New York is a fun city. It's really the future.'

I had seen the future and it stank.

Eventually, more by luck than good judgement, I found my way out and drove 'upstate'. All of America is built around the motor car. Six-lane express ways go straight through a vast countryside. I stopped at a motel and slept.

Next morning, bright and early, I went outside. Nothing could have been more different after the dark dismay of New York. It was autumn, fall, and I had never seen trees and colours like this in my life. Not only trees but a continuous rich rolling carpet of reds, golds, yellows and greens which stretched as far as the eye could see. Some of the first white settlers came from where I live in Suffolk. Flat Suffolk where the horizon and the sky melt into a diffuse mist. Suffolk with some copses, even some large woods, but nothing like this.

I began to understand the contrast they must have felt with their flat homeland and the almost mystical reverence with which the settlers held this newly discovered land. It is beautiful beyond the singing of it.

So you get into your car drunk with the fresh, woody smells, sights and colours and you drive and it goes on and on and on. And then you get arrested for speeding.

It was all too perfect, the road slashing through the hills and colours. The clear sky, the undulating landscape. At first I thought the winking lights were part of the dazzling colours, until the trooper stepped out on to the road and flagged me down. Up to that point in time he had been involved with a coloured kid in a more than averagely battered car. He turned to him, 'You can go.'

The youth looked at him in disgust, 'Shit man, why you hassle us?'

The policeman ignored him.

'Licence!'

I handed him my driving licence.

'Follow me.'

Inside the patrol car, while he studied my licence, I studied the patrol car. It had a two-way and a citizen's band radio, various buttons to stop and start the plethora of lights, horns and sirens. It had a small arsenal tucked discreetly but handily away and the rest of the space was taken

106

up by an immensely sophisticated radar assembly. This was designed so that the trooper could park his car, turn the radar beam in the requisite direction, front, backwards, forwards, switch on and then wait. If a motorist exceeded the speed limit then the very expensive machinery sounded an alarm, flashed the speed on a panel, gave a digital print-out of maximum speed and took a picture of the car and its number plate. All very efficient. Where does the money come from to buy and maintain all this equipment? Why, from mugs like me.

'I must warn you that you have a right to a defence counsel before you say anything.'

I was now in the office of the Town Justice, Floyd 'Deke' Merritt of Kirkwood, N.Y. He had been sitting peacefully on the porch of his office/home when we arrived.

'What's the charge, Trooper Brady?'

'He was doing seventy-six miles an hour.'

'Guilty or not guilty?'

I had not the faintest idea. 'Guilty if you say so.'

'Did you see the signs, the speed restriction signs, fifty-five miles an hour?'

I had tried to ignore all the signs and bill boards, which were obscenities on a peaceful landscape. Rooms to rent, cars to buy, food to eat, fruit to munch, sweets to chew, resorts to rest in, boards advertising boards to advertise on, all repeated *ad nauseam*.

'Did you see them?'

'Yes.'

'Well, ever since the energy crisis we have had a speed limit and the President has decided that so much energy was being saved that he kept the speed limit on.'

In New York they turn the office lights on all night, deifying the concrete monstrosities, but that's business.

'Anything to say?'

'I'm not used to your speed limits, Your Honour.'

'You English?'

'Yes ... sir.'

How does one address a small town sheriff/judge. Sir? Your Honour? Your Worship? Buddy?

A long pause. Anglo-American friendship might just be reaffirmed. As a friendly alien I would be let off with a warning.

'One hundred dollars.'

I paid, smiling manfully.

'Thank you,' I said as I laid out the money. Now I was nearly broke.

Then surprisingly we were all friends.

'Well, that's the beginning,' said Trooper Brady cheerfully, his belly bulging over his gun belt. 'Get a lot this week, it's race week, Deke.'

'Oh Jesus,' groaned the overworked Judge Deke Merritt.

'We've booked Stirling Moss three times,' said Brady with relish, 'three times.'

When they say fifty-five miles an hour they mean it. On to Watkins, past signs that read 'Elect Jerome K. Tolmer for Sheriff. Your pal Jerry.'

Watkins Glen is a little town on the tip of the finger lakes. These lakes, small, but of great beauty, are connected to the Great Lakes. Watkins Glen, like a thousand other small towns on the eastern seaboard, has white wooden houses, straight roads and churches which are conspicuous by their use. The rich are respectable and the poor invisible, or almost so. It is a satisfied, ordered town. One particular road leads out of town and climbs a large hill. The town drops breathtakingly away and suddenly you can see the tops of thousands of other tree-clad hills rolling away in the distance. Then you come to Watkins Glen race track, 'Home of Road Racing in America'. They used to race through the streets years ago, but no longer.

There is only one industry in Watkins – racing. This being race week everyone was doing something to help the dollars roll in. I was clearly not much of an asset to the community. I telephoned England for more money. American technology sprang into action. Telegraphs here, radios there, computers everywhere. The lines hummed, the airways tingled, the programmes spun and . . . nothing happened. My money arrived in Watkins but was rerouted and lost. For some three weeks a large sum of my money was magically held by some ultra-fast computer and tossed around in limbo while various bank officials assured me that yes, it had been sent off, yes it had been received and no, they did not know where it was now. In some forgotten terminal changed on a time-share basis into a binary casualty. Letters finally sorted it out. Who knows, in my old age a repentant, mildewed computer might suddenly spew out my money before it is finally disconnected.

After some miserable days a fellow countryman lent me some money. My banker's card and my Eurocheques were as nothing in the stern eyes of Mike Burke, chief cashier of the Watkins Glen National Bank and Trust Company.

Why not ask the race organisers for a loan he suggested? It is difficult to explain but most race organisers regard writers as rip-off artists par excellence. I had literally to beg for a press pass, which pleased Bob Kelly, the press organiser in some misbegotten puritan way, immensely. He also, with some relish and considerable boorishness was able to refuse me a pass to take photographs. For that I had to be a photographer.

'But,' I explained, 'I am.'

'You said you were a writer,' he observed.

'I'm both.'

'You can't be.' And he dismissed me.

Since I was also there doing a feature article with pictures for a glossy magazine this complicated my life a little. The art editor complained later, 'Where are the close-ups of the racing cars?'

'Not allowed near enough to take them.'

'But didn't you explain . . . ?'

Yes, I did explain. Bob Kelly, take a holiday race week, you plainly need it.

At the track my lack of some passes was accepted with equanimity at first.

'You'll be getting the passes tomorrow. Fine by me ole buddy. Mind how you go.'

The racing teams had all arrived by now and were uncrating their racers and repairing those that had been damaged in Mosport at the race a week previously. The atmosphere of the track was totally different to that of the town. At the track there was an international atmosphere, with Italians, Brazilians, Britons and Americans focusing their attentions on the drivers, the cars and ultimately the race. I interviewed those people I needed to and was slagged off by James Hunt on the telephone.

'Hello, may I speak to James Hunt?'

'Who is that speaking?' In his precise public school accent.

'It's Ronnie Mutch, you remember we arranged . . . '

'Jesus Christ, can't a person get any sleep around here, do you realise what time it is?'

'Eight o'clock . . . '

But the phone was dead.

At the same motel I tried to telephone Niki; the switchboard operator would not put me through.

'Mr Lauda is sleeping, he cannot be disturbed.'

He really does take his sleeping seriously.

I arranged to speak to the Chief Medical Officer. I met Dr John C. Herrman, M.D., in the sheriff's office at the track. I was looking for a white-coated doctor. A man wearing a sheriff's uniform with handcuffs and revolver introduced himself.

'Hi, glad to meet you. John C. Herrman, M.D.'

If ever there was a perfect symbol of America this was it, the doctor with a gun.

'I carry a sidearm because it facilitates communication between me and any law enforcement officers who will naturally be present at any disaster.'

When I averred that he could also say with some force

110

to a patient, 'Get better or else,' he did not smile.

He spoke at length about the medical facilities at Watkins Glen. These facilities are very good indeed, with immediate care for all injuries and then larger hospitals nearby to which the patients can be transferred for long-term treatment or major surgery. He and all other doctors and personnel offered their services free.

'You see I'm not a race buff, the object for me is to pull this thing off administratively.'

In conclusion we discussed guns. Dr Herrman revealed that when he went out at night he changed the .38 for a .357 Magnum. For those readers who do not know, the .357 Magnum is a pistol of immense size and terrifying fire-power. If you hit a man in the shoulder the bullet will rip the whole arm and shoulder off.

'You wear a Magnum in Watkins?' I asked incredulously.

'You never know,' he replied.

And I thought that *I* was paranoid!

Back to the race cars; more tuning then the first practice. It was wet and by now all the world's press had arrived. We were handed a detailed programme with an hourly breakdown of events over the next five days. The programme was the culmination of a year's organisation by Mal Currie, the Race Director. The first two days involved registration and inspection of the circuit. Small beer, everything went more or less to plan except I heard one driver being turned back at a gate.

'But I'm driving in the fuckin' race,' he shouted.

His friend calmed him down and they made for another gate. The best laid plans of mice and men are filed away somewhere.

Friday was practice for Formula One cars and a whole host of subsidiary races. By now the people were coming into the track in droves. The Americans, in their large mobile homes with motorcycles strapped on the back. Watkins filled to bursting and motels seventy miles away were used. Some people, more adventurous or more hardy than

111

the rest, camped near the track. There was some rain and some fog, but not overmuch for the season of mists and mellow fruitfulness.

At the track the pace had started to hot up. Racing is, despite what some say, the ultimate mechanical blood sport. The thin division between brilliance and catastrophe is maintained only through the attention, care and skill of drivers, designers and mechanics. So at trackside the designers, now having largely nothing to do, were nervous, while the mechanics concentrated more acutely and the drivers became more businesslike. The drivers, even though it was a practice, pushed themselves very hard. There were huge rooster tails of spray as the cars roared around. More adjustments, more hurried alterations.

'You never have enough time to do everything you want, that is why you must be as precise as possible about tuning the chassis.' Niki Lauda. Niki's car, because of the crash, was not running exactly to his satisfaction. Hunt and Scheckter turned in the best times on the Friday practice. This timing is done electronically to a thousandth of a second.

'Sometimes it's a thousandth of a second that gets pole position.' Between Hunt with the best practice time and Niki in fifth place, there was not quite one second's difference. You do not win by large margins. 'What we are looking for is a one per cent advantage . . . '

After a race lasting about two hours the time difference between the first four will generally be within ten seconds.

Niki concentrated hard and the swarm of Ferrari mechanics and technicians readjusted the car. But still it was not right. He did not shout or alter his generally impassive demeanour.

'Oversteer, oversteer, we can't get rid of oversteer,' was the closest he came to impatience.

The engine was fine, but the polish necessary in road-holding was not there.

Consider the following. Once a set of tyres has been

112

agreed on, or given by Goodyear (i.e. wet or dry) then you must get your car to go around the track so that it is *absolutely* on the limit, all the time. Anything less than this and a hungry Hunt, Scheckter, Depailler or Andretti (especially Andretti, everyone wants to win on their home ground and Mario Andretti had not yet done this) will very soon pass you. This means that you have to push it to the limit, the fastest it can go, on every corner, all the time. Less than this and you are not a winner, let alone world champion. Tyre pressures must be correct, but a tyre heats up altering this pressure after a while, which alters the parameters in the suspension geometry, which changes how fast you can push it. Also, as fuel is used the car lightens up and any correction in handling to make the car handle well with a full tank can result in disastrous steering problems as the car lightens. This was the area that Niki was working on. Changing this, altering that, stiffen, slacken, loosen, lighten until the right compromise is reached. It must be a compromise because it must be good at the beginning of the race and the end, which are two totally different conditions. This is why when Niki is not racing he is testing. Now he was fit from his accident (although some small doubts remained in people's minds and indeed in Niki's) but the car was new and not right. However, there was another practice day, the chassis would come into tune, Niki would push hard and he would be up with James Hunt in pole position for this very fast track.

By now most of the spectators had arrived and were viewing the cars and sampling the side shows. The grounds and track were damp, but not impossibly so. Saturday was the final big day for adjustment and practice. Trial practice, more hoopla, camera competitions and the Vintage Car Grand Prix. The penultimate build-up to the race.

Then it rained. Not ordinary rain, but the Grand Prix of rains. Big, hard, solid drops that dropped in a downpour so thick that visibility was reduced to a few feet. Everybody, no matter what their clothing, was wet, soggy and miserable.

The campers sat glumly inside their own personal dams of water and outside it rained and rained. The earth was churned up by the mobile homes, trucks, trailers, cars and spectators. The race area, with mud *really* knee deep, started to take on the aspects of a nightmare re-creation of Verdun. Where there was no mud there were vast lakes of impassable water. All the magic moments that should have happened drowned silently. Silently except for the trackside loudspeakers which chanted out monotonously, 'There is a one hundred per cent chance of rain *all day*.'

Inside the only dry attraction, the technical area that housed the racers, the crowd thickened till they were locked solid, unable to move back, forwards or sideways; unable to see the cars or the occasional racer. All this they bore stoically. The radio announcer became increasingly gloomy. Inside the organisers' area there was mounting hysteria, which all funnelled itself sharply on to Mal Currie, the Race Director.

'Mal, the radio is broadcasting that because of the weather the big race has been cancelled. Advising travellers to go back home.' Grey with tension and fatigue Mal looked like a man about to announce Armageddon.

'Tell them it's wrong.'

'Mal, what are we going to do . . .'

'Mal, I can't . . .'

'Mal, it's impossible . . .'

He earned his money many times over that day. Only Jody Scheckter and James Hunt were happy.

'Well, my time is O.K.' Jody.

'You never have enough time for a perfect practice. I'm happy.' James.

The entrance tunnel to the track disappeared under water. Stories drifted into a bored press room about the dangerous denizens of the bog.

'They smoke dope an' all, give racing a bad name,' as one reporter said while we surveyed a ruined racing car left over from Friday's practice.

The bog is peculiar to Watkins. If Watkins Glen is respectable, the bog and the people who go there are quite the opposite. They do smoke dope, they do drink, they do fornicate, they do steal and they have one hell of a good time. The bog is a hollow which is muddy under normal conditions. Legend has it that someone rode a motorcycle through it on a bet and then followed this by taking through a car. He made it on the first run but stuck on the second. The disgruntled driver got out and tossed a match into the car, thus starting a tradition.

The denizens of the bog steal cars, rush them at the mud, and when they stall put them to the torch. Not too long ago a large coach dropped off the Brazilian contingent at the stands and then got lost near the bog (not difficult to do). The driver asked the way. Well, it was difficult, but if he would get out they would try and help him. While bog people were confusing the driver further, someone got into the driver's seat and drove the coach to the bog. It got through on the first pass and stuck on the second. So the coach was burnt. Unfortunately, it also contained all the Brazilians' luggage for a week. The fire fighting trucks keep away from the incinerations for fear that they will be waylaid and burnt as well. This year the festivities started off with a Chev as the first sacrifice.

There were rumours in the press room that the rain had made the people of the bog truculent and that the riot police were on standby. A pleasurable tingle ran through the press corps. In the middle of a riot, what great copy: the Pulitzer prize was within reach.

'As long as those suckers don't cut the telephone wires.'

The tingle subsided and the rain eased off. At some points the race track was now under a foot of water. The possibility of cancellation loomed large.

'What we going to do about the water on the track, Mal?'

'They are digging drainage trenches on the side to let the water run off.'

'For Chrissake how long will that take? The drivers must know.'

'I don't know,' with admirable restraint.

Two drivers went around the track a couple of times but the rain and poor visibility precluded any real practice. I decided to drive back to Watkins to dry out and then see James Hunt. My car was in a lake of water and because I had forgotten to switch off the lights that I needed in the morning's gloom, my battery was flat. American cars are wholly automatic, and rely on electricity to start. Without that you are stymied. I stepped resolutely out of the dry car, into the rain and a lake. The day was not going well. Fortunately, this being Watkins, there was another battery and two jumper leads close at hand.

Simultaneously with me, all other spectators seemed to want to get the hell out of the soaked race track. A traffic jam of epic proportions developed. I sat in the car and listened to the radio. It is not so much that Americans are saturated with advertisements, it is just that the break in the continuous hard sell is a bit disconcerting. The traffic began to move. The women in the cars in front of me were behaving strangely. Startled, blushing, angry. There were two people at the side of the road with a large printed sign. The sort which I presumed read 'Lift to New York please'. Nothing to get upset about. I drew level. In the next car was an unsmiling woman. The sign was turned around. 'Show us your tits,' it read. I thought she was going to drive straight into the bogpersons.

Eventually I arrived at James's motel. He was also having problems.

'One hamburger, please.'

'You can't order hamburgers after five.'

James blinked in disbelief.

'But that is the only thing that you serve that is worth eating here.'

This at the grandest motel, or Motor Inn as it now calls itself, in Watkins.

116

'What can I have then?'

'You can't have anything between five and six.'

James reddened slightly. 'Do you mean to say *I* can't have anything.'

The waitress looked at him and then conceded, 'Well, seeing as how it's *you*, as a special favour . . . ' She produced a large menu.

'Hamburger,' said James promptly.

'No hamburgers,' said the waitress smiling.

James lectured her severely on the culinary customs of Spain where he now lives ' . . . and,' he concluded, 'you can get a snack at any time.'

'Different countries, different customs,' she said snapping closed her order book and walking smartly away.

'Hassle,' said James. 'Bloody hassle all the time.'

We spoke a while then I left for the town. It was still raining, the only film theatre in town was showing an 'Adult', i.e. blue movie. I decided to taste American beer instead. It was a foolish choice.

The tavern had a full selection of all the available beers, Schlitz, Budweiser, Coors, Genesee and so on. Sampling all these beers is like listening to the entire 'Ring of the Niebelung,' without the funny bits.

My warm local in Suffolk, The Compasses, with its rolypoly landlord (with a kind word for all) and landlady became painful by its absence, as I drank more cold, fizzy water and washing up liquid. Oh Adnams! Oh Abbot! Oh God! I went to bed.

The next morning, race day, was miraculously clear. A few fluffy clouds, but not a hint of yesterday's deluge in the sky. A bracing autumn day. The track was dry.

Because of the pressure of time a number of events were abandoned and the racing began. But not before an interdenominational early morning service at the track, this being America and Sunday. With Catholics, Protestants, Jews, Holy Rollers (driving the Rizla Penthouse no less) and petrol from the land of the Prophet the option on prayer

117

combinations must have been interesting. The subsidiary races were run quickly and efficiently and then came the main event. The F1 Grand Prix. A warm up lap and mechanics, with a half an hour before the big test, working frantically on last minute alterations. Stirling Moss, now the grand old man of racing and presumably booked for the fourth time in Kirkwood, walked around giving advice to selected drivers. All the drivers had qualified to race. On the sidelines Chris Amon with bones broken a week previously hobbled around on crutches, a grim reminder of what happens when things go just slightly wrong at high speed.

The track was cleared, engines started again and they moved up to the starting grid. Revs up, noise up, tension up to breaking point and suddenly on the sunlit track they were away in a shimmering haze of heat, smoke and burnt rubber.

Scheckter was the first to emerge from the corner with Hunt just behind him. Niki was in a bunch just behind them. Because of the cancelled practice session, Scheckter had called for some major adjustments on his car and had not been able to test them before he raced. His first corner on his own admission could have been his last.

'I just went into that corner and hoped for the best.'

Whatever else one might think, there is a great deal of skill and courage involved in an act such as this. Lauda with cool precision chopped his way past the two racers in front of him, Ronnie Petersen and Vittorio Brambilla. The latter is a feat not to be underrated, since Brambilla is not exactly well known for reliability.

The time interval between the first three was then some 2.5 and 6 seconds respectively. This held for a while with Hunt pushing Scheckter very hard indeed. Down the pit straight they thundered, then on the line for the first corner. Hunt, in the beginning, consistently drifted off the track and on to the warning kerb bubbles that signal to the driver that the end of the track, and the race, is at hand. He did this every lap to begin with because the car was oversteering and

118

because to come out of a corner very fast you have to go in very fast. This was hard racing and good judgement. There was one minor accident involving Arturo Merzario, and some retirements. Then on lap fourteen Jacky Ickx came out of the fast straight in his Ensign (Amon had also injured himself in an Ensign) and into a left-handed bend. He kept on going, into the Armco barrier. The front end of his racer sheared itself off at the barrier and burst into flames, while the rest of the car and Ickx rebounded back into the middle of the track. The flames roared and the fire marshals instantly played their extinguishers over Ickx. He released himself from the ruin that once was a racer and walked trance-like off the track as the front half of his car died in flame. The cars flashed past the flame and the debris. Niki saw the flames, did this not cause a stab of terror, a slight slowing up?

'You watch for the flags, if there are no flags and no pieces on the track, you race.'

Some of the racers did slow down for a while, but the track was cleared and the race continued. Ickx was hospitalised with a broken ankle.

Scheckter at the halfway point seemed to be running into steering problems as he gunned the racer round the track, holding it in line at times with what looked like sheer brute force. Hunt's car was losing the oversteer as it lightened and the tyres gripped as they got really hot. He waited for his chance and then took Jody at the chicane which Jody had designed. The crowd responded with a roar that really came from the heart. Then James was baulked by a backmarker, missed a gear and Jody swept by again after two laps. Niki dropped further back now. He was having to cope with increasing handling problems from his Ferrari. He was getting huge oversteer, but to the outsider, because of his precision, it simply looked as though the magic had gone from his driving.

'If I pushed it harder, I lose it. This is foolish.'

With twelve laps to go Hunt pulled past Scheckter again

119

and put his foot down. He opened a gap of eight seconds in twelve laps, which is not bad going, Niki persisted but it was not good enough. On the last lap, Hunt's team mate, Mass, challenged Niki for third place. With just the requisite effort Niki came third by .134 of a second. Thus are points and world championships won and lost.

With more practice time and more chassis tuning, Niki would undoubtedly have been up with the two leaders, fighting at every corner, contesting every thousandth of a second.

And suddenly on that autumn afternoon the race was over and they led Lauda, Scheckter and Hunt to the winners' podium. Champagne, Coke, cigarettes and laurels for James, smiles all round. James, red in the face from exertion and concentration, his blond hair matted by sweat, was the centre of attention. Niki and Jody stood by while speeches were made and the pictures taken. But the fans only want the winner. So they grabbed, pulled, touched, tugged and asked James dumb questions as he had said they would. Niki slipped away.

'My business is racing and I am tired, I go now.'

He was happy for James in his win, but more preoccupied with the problems he was having with his car.

The crowd swelled around James. He smiled all the while, a perfect winner. Then there was the press conference and the usual post race exhilaration and chaos. The journalists hammered out their deadlines and above the clicking metallic din a frantic official shouted for quiet.

'Yes, it's disgusting all these journalists working in the press office, stop this immediately,' joked Hunt.

Laughter, noise and more questions. James emerged from the press office and a motley gang of fans followed him to the Goodyear marquee. They waved Union Jacks and sang 'Rule Britannia' with more gusto than tune. Some were wearing moth-eaten top hats and moth-eaten tails. All ages and sexes, they were deliriously happy with James. Then something rather odd happened to me. Although I was writing a book on Niki, I, too, felt very proud of being British, which strictly speaking, I am not. A small, dirty, be-whiskered bogdweller accosted me.

'You British?'

'Yes.'

'That James Hunt, man, wow!'

'Yes . . . '

'You know I been there, Oxford, you know it? Man, it's real neat. So neat man I'm jus' goin' to go back there. Have a drink.'

I drank some upstate New York Burgundy from the bottle and felt rather good. It had been a good race and *we* had won. Pity about Niki though.

X

Winners and Losers

I returned and saw that under the sun, the race is not to the swift, nor the battle to the strong . . . but time and chance happeneth to them all. Ecclesiastes 9:11.

The race is sure as hell not going to the World Championship Racers. Bernie Ecclestone 16.12.76.

As I write this it is winter in Europe and there is a very slight pause in the tempo of racing. Some cars and racers are on the Paul Ricard track in France, testing. Ferrari are going hard at it in Modena on their new models and in South America, they are working hard on the Copersucars. Even Japan will be testing their F1 entry and Niki will have had one more operation to enable him to close his eye properly. He and James are also collecting various trophies all over the world, for courage and winning, respectively.

Tall, elegant Marlene will not be inhaling nervously on a cigarette in the pits as she waits for the moment she enjoys best, when the race is over. She will in this short breathing space around Christmas, be practising her hobbies, 'photography and life', so this last chapter is not on how to drive and win, but on the bits and pieces that go towards making a complete picture. The bits that are the main concern of everyday life.

There was some doubt whether there would be a Formula One Grand Prix season at all, because of the dispute between the constructors' association (F.I.C.A.) and the newly formed World Championship Racers. When is a contract not a contract? What is a diffuse declaration of intent? It is on such niceties that Max Mosley and Bernie Ecclestone are haggling with the Argentinians. The season seems to be grinding on to its inevitable fuck ups. So let us leave the arena and look at some of the quieter moments in the racing drivers' lives.

Marlene, who would no doubt look attractive in an old sack, is the daughter of an artist, born in Curaçao. She has travelled and lived just about everywhere, which may account for her easy adjustment to the peripatetic existence of a racing driver. Like other drivers, Niki travels and then gets into a mental routine some time before a race and, as mentioned, when the race comes nearer is not all that approachable. Marlene at this point melts into the background. It was during this period that I was able to speak at length to her on Niki and life.

'Being a world champion has not changed anything for Niki or for me,' she said. As I interviewed her, three photographers were focusing and snapping away and another newspaperman was noting all her replies. Ho hum.

Niki: 'I can't go out anywhere without people asking for an autograph. If I go out for coffee it is autographs. So I stay at home.'

He has in fact perfected a technique of signing autographs automatically, without pausing in conversation, or losing concentration on what he was doing. Marlene views living with the iron-willed Niki as very easy. Because of her own strong will? I asked. 'Oh no I am not strong willed.' Yet a little while later there was a brief argument in which not more than ten words were exchanged. It was perfectly obvious that this was a clash of temperaments on an epic scale. Marlene walked out slightly red and controlling her anger. Niki continued talking about the car.

'No photographs now,' she told a cameraman. 'Perhaps later.'

She did not however intrude on Niki's major preoccupation – his racing car.

There are various views on racing drivers' wives, from team managers, 'Bloody nuisances, always pushing their noses in everywhere' . . . to mechanics, 'Wives, yes, they're all right, see mine once a month or so . . . oh *his* wife, didn't know he had one' . . . to the drivers themselves, 'It is hard for the women.' Carlos Pace, killed early in the season.

'Pam's the one who really has to put up with a lot,' Jody Scheckter.

James Hunt: 'Suzy got married in good faith, wanted to settle down, have a full relationship and all that and I mistakenly thought I could do that. As soon as I got married it was plain that I couldn't and the racing was heavy because I was rushing about trying to get on with a career and Suzy wanted to be at home. When she stayed at home she was lonely and when she came with me I moved too fast for her 'cos I was working and I would miss aeroplanes and things so it was doomed. Drivers' wives either sit at home and breed or get bored. There seems no easy way out of this one. One way to avoid it is not to get married, I knew this but I had to check it out. You see, Suzy is the sweetest girl you could ever meet, which is, I suppose, why I married her and when things started to go wrong I was delighted that she met Richard. He really is a nice guy, you media people made him out to be some sort of a monster but he isn't, he's just very nice which is why I'm glad for him and glad for Suzy and not at all jealous. The fact that I was failing to fulfil my responsibilities to her was a source of conscience and aggravation to me. They're very happy. I see them both from time to time and we are all very friendly.'

There is an aura about the Grand Prix drivers that is undeniably attractive – the flirtation with death, the machismo image of racing (there was one woman G.P. driver, Leila Lombardi, but she never really got anywhere), which makes the drivers undoubtedly attractive to women.

Niki: 'Before I was married I had girls, yes. *I* always chose them. But now I am a good married man.'

Some of the other drivers were more circumspect, a glance around the room to see where the wife was, then a discreet cough, 'Well, of course if you are away from home and a pretty girl is talking to you, then yes . . . I am human.'

James Hunt: 'A race starts for me on Thursday evening. I'm into a strict routine by then and I don't have time for women, but like this afternoon, with the rain, I'd rather be screwing than gassing to you. You have to do something on a rainy day and it's a nice distraction and a nice relaxation, but it can't really be a serious thing because I'm busy and because it has to be on my terms, it can't be really nice for them. I'm too busy racing you see.'

Woman, glowing: 'Mario was so nice to me, he spoke to me . . . '

Husband, drily: 'That's because he's got the hots for you.'

With all the travel involved (for which, incidentally, the top twenty finishers in any G.P. race get recompensed totally by the race organiser), the teams do not spend much time at home or at any fixed base.

James Hunt: 'I have a home in Marbella but I very seldom get back there, which is a bit of a drag.'

Carlos Pace: 'I have a home in London where my children are at present. No, I do not see them enough.'

Niki Lauda, somewhat sourly: 'Yes, someone looks after my house when I am not there. They use it more than I do.'

James Hunt: 'I have a housekeeper called Anita and she is rather dishy,' he paused, 'but she is strictly a housekeeper. It doesn't pay to fraternise with the staff. It leads to aggravation and always ends in a big pain in the arse. That's the point of having a housekeeper and not a wife, isn't it? If you're going to sleep with your housekeeper you may as well make her your wife.'

The life of a world champion, open to constant importuning from fans, almost by definition restricts the number of true friends one has. Many years ago, world champion

Juan Fangio described his friends. In his warm Latin way, they included the entire village where he was born and brought up. He also defined what he meant by friendship, 'It is obligation without bounds on both sides.' The villagers at the start of Fangio's career all chipped in to buy him his first real racer. Niki by contrast does not have a great many friends, indeed according to his rigorous definition, he does not have any.

Niki: 'I do not know what a friend is. In motor racing you have a lot of friends when you win. You have no friends when you lose. The friends you have when you lose are only there because they think you will win again. What is a friend? A friend is someone who lives for you day and night and vice versa. I would not be able to do this so I have no friends, I am handicapped by my job.'

And Marlene?

'That is different, she is my wife. I married her because I loved her and she loves me. She is strong like me. But this is love not friendship.'

Niki's views on friendship may make him sound like a very cold man, but he is not. It is as well to remember that during the season the world champion has to put up with an incredible number of demands on his time, energy and attention. To expect a man to have a gaggle of friends as well is perhaps a little too much. On top of this is one dominant fact. Niki when I spoke to him had just come through a most terrifying, near fatal accident. The mind and the body in many small ways take years to heal. If he was suddenly big news because of his near death, who can blame him if he erects barriers in life?

Niki is still very visibly and horribly scarred on his face by his accident. This certainly does not bother Marlene one jot. For her the essential Niki is still totally there. And that, for her, is what matters completely.

Part of Niki has not changed ever since he started racing. His racing ability. This, he maintains, was always there. What has changed is the accumulated experience on which he now draws. But was there never any point at which his ability was at variance with his ambition?

The answer is a very simple, 'No'.

Having achieved his ambition, he is proud, but quietly so and overall he is modest, almost embarrassingly so; this leads to some conflict with fans who misinterpret his modesty and need for privacy as standoffishness, not in the superstar mould.

'I do not regard myself as a superstar. I leave that to you people. I have achieved what I set out to do, become world champion F1 driver, but the rest I am not very interested in, that is the bullshit side.' It is partly this which led to an incident which James Hunt commented on:

'Niki was in the paddock when a fan of his came up and gave him a scrap book which he had collected together. Niki simply took the book and said, "Yes, now go." Even if the book was bloody awful, which is certainly was, I think Niki should have taken it, given the kid a smile and some chat. I would have. They, the fans, make us what we are, you know.'

James, however, does enjoy the limelight a great deal more than Niki. So with Niki the questions tend to focus on the more technical aspect of racing and inevitably his accident. What was he most grateful for afterwards?

'That I was not permanently damaged in any way.'

Did he subsequently ever think of stopping racing?

'No, when I survived I had to race again because you build up experience over four or five years and then if you stop you lose it and you can't start again. So I did not think at all of stopping. Psychologically I had to find out whether I could continue though.'

For him now there is really no end of season, a slackening perhaps, a slowing down of pace, but never a halt.

'There is no end of season. On the last race I have to go to Modena to test the new car for the next season. The last race is in October, the first race is in January in Argentina. In between there is work.'

127

What will he do when he drives his last race, when he retires?

'I don't know because I am one hundred per cent adjusted to motor racing. If I could find something which interested me more I would quit, this has not happened yet.'

In the last race in Japan the conditions were very dangerous. With one world championship in the bag already and trouble with his eye in the mist and rain Niki did not think the race worth the risk. James Hunt, who had not yet won a world championship, did not agree with Niki. This was no needle match; Niki very carefully weighed up the possibilities and in his view the risks outweighed the advantages.

'You must remember it is me who in the end takes the decisions – I am the driver.'

Because James Hunt led from the start of the race, no one else had his clear view. They were driving completely blind in the leader's rooster tail, at speeds in excess of 150 m.p.h. It does take a great deal of unsung courage to do that. Also, although Niki would dispute this, James had luck. (In the selection of British army officers, this factor, luck, is taken into account. 'Not very good but he did have luck and every good general also has luck, let him in.') Luck in many ways, luck that one tyre lasted precisely as long as it did, luck that most of the others changed tyres at the wrong time, luck that the rain stopped when it did and perhaps most breathtakingly luck that the doyen of shunters, Brambilla, lost it and spun just an inch away from him but did not touch him.

Not only Niki adjudged the race too dangerous, so did Fittipaldi, twice world champion and very experienced in these matters. So did Carlos Pace and Larry Perkins.

The season is over but there will be other races for Niki and Ferrari and the rest of the brave Grand Prix gladiators. When you see them flash by, remember what Niki said, 'We human beings have many more resources of the spirit which we do not use. I try to use them.'